A Holistic Vision of
the Human Adventure

at the Edges
of Life

A Holistic Vision of
the Human Adventure

at the Edges
of Life

Bruce G. Epperly

Chalice Press

St. Louis, Missouri

All scripture quotations, unless otherwise indicated, are from the *New Revised Standard Version Bible*, copyright 1989, Division of Christian Education of the National Council of the Churches of Christ in the USA. Used by permission.

Scripture quotations marked Phillips are reprinted with permission of Macmillan Publishing Co., Inc., from *The New Testament in Modern English*, Rev. Edn., translated by J.B. Phillips. © J.B. Phillips, 1958, 1960, 1972.

Cover design: Will Hardin

Art Director: Michael A. Dominguez

Library of Congress Cataloging–in–Publication Data

Epperly, Bruce Gorden.
   At the edges of life: a holistic vision of the human adventure/ by Bruce G. Epperly.
ISBN 0-8272-0020-X
1. Death—Religious aspects—Christianity. 2. Holistic medicine—Religious aspects—Christianity. 3. Christian life—
1960–. 4. Process theology. I. Title
BT825.E677 1992   236'.1   92-19073

Printed in the United States of America

Contents

Foreword by John B. Cobb, Jr.   vii

Preface   xi

1 Introduction:
    Adventure at the Edges of Life   1

2 From Despair to Transformation   9

3 The Dying-Rising God   43

4 Death and Our Images
    of Health   67

5 Christian Theology and
    the Recovery of Healing   111

6 Death and Spirituality   137

7 Epilogue:
    Adventure and Immortality   159

Foreword

Ever since Luther, Protestant theologians have prided themselves on rejecting the theology of glory in favor of the theology of the cross. Since the eighteenth century, they have prided themselves also on limiting their affirmations to what makes sense in relation to the modern worldview. As a result, the oldline Protestant churches have provided diminished excitement, enthusiasm, and comfort.

Popular movements in our culture have renewed the theology of glory in many forms. Some have been explicitly Christian. Christian Science, New Thought, the power of positive thinking, Pentecostalism, and the charismatic movement come to mind. Some have given up on Christianity. A cluster of religious movements that can be loosely grouped as "new age" play a not insignificant role in contemporary society. The breakdown of the authority of "modern" ways of thinking has released energies that support these new approaches.

Fundamentalism and liberalism spend much of their energy attacking each other. But their reactions to these enthusiastic movements have often been quite similar. They see them as failing to express the gospel of the crucified one. Both fundamentalists and liberals cling to much of the "modernity" to which they have adapted themselves even after the categories of modernity have shown their inadequacy in the sciences themselves.

Bruce Epperly does not ask us to reject the crucified one and join a new age movement. But he does see—rightly, I believe—that the attitude of condemnation and closure toward the new religious spirit abroad in the land blocks the churches from dealing with important issues. The hunger for a more positive and joyful message, one that promises health and life, is deep-seated, and it is not to be condemned. Jesus was surrounded by persons with these needs, and he looked on them with compassion. Epperly believes that some of those outside the church, who are looking quite freshly at these matters, have much to teach us.

Our commitment to rationality has led us to silence about life after death and even about death itself. And ironically our commitment to the theology of the cross, by directing attention to the cruciform life, has silenced the question of death itself. The results have not been healthy. Ideas about dying and death and what happens after death have become common topics of conversation more outside than within the churches. The absence of the church's voice in these conversations has opened the door to much that has been naive and destructive. The ignoring of all this by the church has further isolated it from the religious concerns and vitality of the culture.

Accordingly, Epperly focuses his discussion on death, and on how our understanding of death, expressed or repressed, shapes our lives. He draws on Christian tradition. But he also draws on the wisdom of the best spokespersons for the current thinking on these matters outside the church. He wants Christians to contribute to those discussions. But he also wants Christians to be open to learn, both what they have forgotten from their own heritage, and what they may never have known.

Our oldline denominations today are losing members and are understandably concerned about their own dying. The dominant mood generated by this fear of dying is one of growing rigidity. The churches are losing the spirit of adventure. They call for evangelism, but they suppose that those to be evangelized are attracted by a conservative and closed spirit. No doubt some are, but these already have plenty of churches to choose among. The desire of the oldline churches to compete for those who are looking primarily for familiarity and security is naive.

A far more promising field for evangelism for the oldline churches would be the millions who have given up on the church because of its narrow horizons and its boring and depressing message. This narrowness and this message belie the good news they profess to express. Many are attracted by local congregations in which there is renewed excitement generated by exploration of new frontiers and openness to learn from all who have something to teach. When they find that the wisdom and liveliness they have had to seek outside the church can be found in the church as well, they joyfully return.

The practical adventure of the church into new fields needs to be preceded by, or at least accompanied by, a new adventure of thinking. Epperly calls for this adventure and guides us into it. It goes against the grain of many "modern" Christians. No doubt, like all experiments and risk-taking, it makes its share of errors. If it claimed to be a comprehensive theology, most of us would say that the notes of penitence and sacrifice are too much subordinated. But when viewed against the massive neglect of much that has been important to the Christian faith in its times of real vitality, it is, at the very least, a healthy corrective. And the spirit it breathes is far more holy than the institutionalism and defensiveness that dominate our denominations.

John B. Cobb, Jr.
Claremont, California

Preface

My mother died unexpectedly last year. For some reason, on the anniversary of her death I am drawn to the homeland of my ancestors. On the surface I seek to explore the territory of the MacMillan clan of which my mother's family is a part. Yet, something deeper is drawing me to the western coast of Scotland, described by novelist Paul Theroux in his *The Kingdom by the Sea* as having a "paradoxical beauty—its landscape was both lovely and severe; it was a monotonous extravaganza. The towns are as dull as any I had ever seen in my life, and the surrounding mountains were very wild. I liked what I saw, but I kept wanting to leave."[1] Prior to my mother's death, my intrigue with living abundantly in the face of death fueled my writing of this book, just as after her death, it fuels my journey to the land of my mother's ancestors. For me, the quest for adventure at the edges of life is personal as well as theological. I seek to discover beauty, meaning, and joy amid the inevitable pain and uncertainty of my own life.

I realize that although "religion is what an individual does with his [or her] solitariness,"[2] I share the search for meaning at the edges of life with countless others whose adventures beyond their known world are inspired by the reality of death in its many guises. The "edges of life" of which I speak are not merely those defined by death, but also those uncharted spiritual territories that beckon us onward. In a time in which an old age seems to be dying and a new age tentatively emerging, we need visions of what it means to live as whole and healthy persons in body, mind, and spirit. If Christian faith is to be meaningful in our time, it must provide imaginative visions for adventurers at the edges of life. I offer this book as a modest guide to those who seek to explore the spiritual frontiers that lure us forward.

As I reflect on the adventure of writing this book, I realize that I stand in the midst of a "cloud of witnesses," whose inspiration has made this book possible. I would like to thank Professor Marie Fox, who first introduced me to Whitehead and the love of philosophy. I am grateful beyond words to Professor John B.

Cobb, Jr., who has over the years been a spiritual and intellectual guide and whose encouragement made this book possible. I would also like to thank Professor Marc Ford for his suggestions and affirmations of the first draft of this work.

To my editor David Polk, I owe a debt of gratitude for his personal and editorial support. None of this would have been possible without the love and friendship of Rev. Kate Gould Epperly, whose creative spirit brought life to my professorial style. To our son Matthew Epperly, I am thankful for the "study breaks" of basketball, baseball, and conversation.

Above all, I thank God for my parents, Loretta Baxter Epperly and Everett Lewis Epperly, whose faith in God and love for me instilled in me the desire to adventure in the seldom traveled paths of the spirit.

Notes

[1] Paul Theroux, *The Kingdom by the Sea* (New York: Houghton-Mifflin, 1983), p. 263.

[2] Alfred North Whitehead, *Religion in the Making* (New York: Macmillan, 1926), p. 16.

1

Introduction: Adventure at the Edges of Life

An ancient legend tells of a man who tried to run away from death. His master had sent him to the bazaar in Baghdad on a business excursion. He returned early from his assignment, trembling and ashen faced. As he fell to his knees before his master, he stammered, "Master, lend me your fastest horse, for I have just seen Death in the marketplace and he threatened me. Tonight, I will ride to Samarra where I will be safe." Being a good man, the master lent him the horse. The servant rode toward safety, looking neither to the right nor to the left. Being a brazen man, the master went to the marketplace in search of Death. When he found Death, he challenged him: "Why did you frighten my servant today?" Death responded, "I did not mean to frighten him. When I saw him, I gave a gesture of surprise. For I have plans to meet him tonight along the road to Samarra!"

We race toward the safety of Samarra. Yet all along the way are reminders that there is no escape and that, whether we like it or not, death is something we must all eventually face. On the surface it appears that our society's denial of death is lessening. Books on death and dying, surviving cancer, holistic health, past lives, and near-death experiences line bookstore shelves. University, seminary, and adult education courses on death and dying attract high enrollments. Once taboo, the subject of death in its many aspects confronts us even in the supermarket checkout lines. We are even beginning to talk publicly about it. With the growing interest in "living wills," some even plan for a deathstyle to match their lifestyle. Yet, ironically, even the recent attempts to see death as a natural event, devoid of stigma and fear, are often just another way to control and domesticate the mysterious and uncontrollable by submitting it to an informational, psychological, and technological "fix." Our society's very attempt to face death may be a subtle form of avoidance and manipulation. As the philosophers Søren Kierkegaard and Martin Heidegger have pointed out, what is known by everyone is seldom understood by anyone. My thesis is that there is much to know about death and that it can be learned in the exploration of life itself at its physical and spiritual edges.

There are good reasons for lay spiritual caregivers and concerned church people, as well as theologians and ministers such as myself, to reflect with some intentionality on the interplay of death, spirituality, and human wholeness. As psychologist Robert Jay Lifton notes, the contemporary age is a period of profound "psychohistorical dislocation."[1] Lifton is right in perceiving that while "the holocausts of twentieth-century warfare have rendered death absurd, the dislocations of the modern world have rendered life's meaning problematic."[2] Amid a growing sense of rootlessness, relativity, and uncertainty about the future, the religious institutions and ritualized forms of behavior that have traditionally given meaning to life are also in crisis. The symbols of immortality and transcendence that have enabled persons throughout the ages to affirm both life and death are in flux, and have lost much of their power to give a meaningful vision of life. In such a spiritual and symbolic void, death has almost become a "lost season," unexpected and meaningless, yet potentially frightening and debilitating. Although a few persons within Christian communities may be well informed about death, this factual knowledge provides little consolation when we face death in its concrete manifestations. Without meaningful symbols of immortality and images of the world in which we live, the edges of life become terrifying and we become desensitized and numbed, distanced from both life and death, unable to feel either the heights or the depths of experience.[3]

The picture appears desolate, but spiritual breakthroughs have always occurred in the context of dislocation and crisis. Meaningful images have arisen to respond to the threats of death, chaos, and meaninglessness. Our time of dislocation and dis-ease need be no exception. In the past, clergy, along with poets, theologians, artists, and mystics, have been the midwives, artisans, and interpreters of these personal and cultural experiences of transcendence and awakening. Today the signs of a spiritual breakthrough are on the horizon, but the traditional religious leaders are not found at the forefront.

When we look at our society we hear the death rattle of once vital, but now irrelevant, images of spirituality, medicine, and healing. We also feel the birth pangs of a new vision of reality and human existence. While the traditional symbols seem to lack relevance and vitality, except to a handful of orthodox believers, there is an emerging panorama of new—and thus far ungrounded—symbols that have sprung forth to fill the void as laypersons everywhere seek to respond to the crisis. Once the interplay of life, death, and human hope was understood in terms of the symbols of heaven and hell, the resurrection and life everlasting, the sacraments and the reign of God; today the edges of human possibility are being investigated in the context of spiritual healing and therapeutic touch, psychic channeling and past lives, reincarnation and astral bodies. Even science, so often identified with materialism and unbelief, is beginning to describe reality in terms of holograms, hidden purposes, and the "cosmic dance" of nature's most basic elements.

However, amid the many emerging images and symbols, there is little synthesis and even less coherence. In this age of novelty and contrast, characterized by the competing and colorful metaphysical claims of "new age" visionaries, the traditional caretakers of human hope within the leadership of the church remain excessively vague and relativistic in their pronouncements. If Lifton is correct in saying that our current repression of mortality is grounded in the interplay of outdated concepts of reality, meaningless symbols, and the distancing from nature characteristic of the technological age, who will respond to the need for an overarching vision to bridge the chasm between traditional and "new age" symbols, practices, and metaphysics? The task requires a creative and inclusive synthesis that is both cosmic and personal in nature. The current challenge to church leaders, theologians, and spiritual caregivers of all perspectives is to reflect upon the personal and spiritual uniqueness of our own time and to discern in partnership with other adventurers at the edges of life what symbols, rituals, and cosmic images most effectively address the needs of our time. In particular, such an exploration must address the ever-present, yet globally repressed, experience of death.

We are filled with a sense of awe and mystery as we reflect on our experience of the edges of life. What does death mean for a society in which both people and animals are removed from the home to die? Why is it that we pay so little attention to the wisdom of the elders and yet feel cheated when we miss the last words of an aged loved one? What does it mean to believe in God's everpresent love, while facing the possibility of terminal cancer or Alzheimer's disease?

Ironically, at a time when persons have little direct contact with death, death in its symbolic forms—global warming and nuclear winter, AIDS and Alzheimer's disease—presents itself to us in a magnitude that dwarfs any previous age. Despite the growing influence of the hospice movement, hospitals and mortuaries have replaced the home as the place of death and dying. The experience of infant mortality and the death of animals is unexpected in the technological age, except in select urban and rural locales. For all that we and our children read and hear about death in the abstract, we seldom see its face except as depersonalized on celluloid. We fear, yet seek, the solace of institutional health care and its arsenal of CAT scans, MRIs, chemotherapy, and transplants. We are constantly "waging war" on cancer, heart disease, AIDS, and other life-threatening illnesses. We follow the progress of recipients of artificial hearts and the health of national leaders, knowing that death lurks ominously in the background. While watching such popular superheroes as Luke Skywalker or the Teenage Mutant Ninja Turtles confront the forces of cosmic darkness, we are humorously distracted from our vague remembrance of the possibility of nuclear holocaust or the slow death of the biosphere from ozone depletion, the razing of rain forests, or oil slicks. We are bombarded to the point of numbness by media blitzes on "safe sex" and drug wars at home, and by news of famine and drought abroad. All this leaves us with a vague and often unarticulated anxiety. We know that death exists. Yet, like the rider to Samarra, we flee from death by psychological repression, superficial conversation, and technical information. If a spiritual breakthrough is to emerge from our personal and cultural encounters with death, it must emerge precisely from confronting our culture's subtle "approach-avoidance" response to mortality.

For those who intentionally embrace the tension of mortality and transcendence, the meeting place of life and death is an invitation to adventure. Although our age may find the identification of death with adventure unusual, the heritage of Christian faith, as well as its current "new age" counterparts, has always understood that the ultimate meaning of life is to be found at its edges. Death is mysterious and frightening but it is not meaningless. From the abandonment and agony of a cross, redemption and new life burst forth. To those who are willing to let go of their grasp on their individual lives, abundant and eternal life is promised.

The mysteries surrounding the edges of life inspire us to new adventure. The metaphor of adventure evokes images of a quest for strange and beckoning lands, a vision of new horizons and expanded awareness, of stretching the limits of the known and discovering the treasures of an unknown land. Since it is always accompanied by a sense of dislocation and uncanniness, adventure calls forth the virtues of courage, endurance, hope, and, foremost, imagination. There is risk, for adventure takes us beyond the familiar. We may feel ourselves homeless and rootless. But as feminist theologian Nelle Morton says, "the journey is home."[4] Along with the risk is the reality that we are challenged to re-birth new visions of ourselves and the known world.

Today, theologians, laypersons, and spiritual caregivers must join hands in the adventure of exploring, naming, and claiming the edges of life so that the crisis of our time will become the opportunity to discover novel images, symbols, and visions that embrace, yet go beyond, the novel techniques and insights emerging in medicine, science, and popular spirituality. This adventure must be global and inclusive in character. It must go beyond familiar Christian parochialisms and stagnant doctrines to embrace the insights and spiritual vitality of Eastern religions, Christian, Native American, and feminist mysticism, as well as the new age movement.

The maps we chart and the metaphors we employ will be tentative and provisional. Nevertheless, they will enable the human spirit to find both comfort and courage as it faces the "many" deaths and the "mini" deaths characteristic of each life lived and every cultural terrain traversed. With the adventure will come the discovery of an ageless spiritual landscape, which needs to be conceptualized anew. With this discovery will come the transformation and revitalization of the traditional metaphors of Christian spirituality.

I wish to assert strongly my conviction that any attempt to venture into the realm of death, dying, and health must integrate and renew the symbols and rituals of traditional Christian faith with the emerging symbols and practices of contemporary medicine, holistic health care, and new age visionaries.[5] We must honor the wisdom of the ancients while pursuing the novelty of the present moment. For clergy and layperson alike, the articulation of an inclusive vision is imperative in our time.

The quest for an inclusive and ecological vision must eventually lead to philosophical reflection. As I reflect on the maps of reality available to us in our time, my perspective as a university chaplain and theologian leads me to believe that the vision of reality conceived by the twentieth-century philosopher Alfred North Whitehead (1861–1947) and his theological followers provides the most promising conceptual framework for the discernment and integration of the varied images of human wholeness emerging in our time.[6] The inclusive and open-ended character of Whitehead's process-relational philosophy addresses the concerns of the physicist and the holistic healer, the mystic and the physician, the theist and the depth psychologist. This "relational" philosophy provides an intellectual and spiritual set of binoculars through which differing images of reality can be viewed together, yielding a new vision, a "creative synthesis," of the many realities seen at the edges of life.

My intention in this book is to sketch out a broad vision of reality and spiritual nurture that animates my own personal search for health and informs my Christian hope for a lively death. My primary concern in these theological reflections is to share perspectives that have enabled me not only "to live" and thus cope with reality, but "to live well and to live better" in the face of all that threatens my spiritual, social, and physical well-being.[7] The ideas that I share in this book are practical as well as theoretical. They have shaped my spiritual journey, my marriage and parenting, as well as my ministry, teaching, and pastoral care. They are at the heart of my own spiritual adventure as a Christian. My orientation is, therefore, pastoral insofar as I explore, dialogue with, and seek to employ in practice new insights in thanatology, spirituality, and holistic medicine.

In the following chapters I employ the insights of Whitehead's process thought in response to concerns found at the edges of life: issues of healthful living as well as lively dying. Chapters two and three focus specifically on the interplay of death and adventure, and articulate a vision of God and human life that enables persons to face the actual as well as symbolic dimensions of death with courage and creativity. Chapters four and five explore images of health and healing in our time and suggest that Whitehead's understanding of the interrelatedness of life can serve as the basis for a holistic vision integrating contemporary medicine, alternative forms of health care, and Christian spirituality. I also explore the concept of spiritual or faith healing in the context of Whitehead's relational image of God. Chapters six and seven explore the organic relationship of death, spiritual development, and the possibility of survival after death.

Throughout this book I am attempting a creative synthesis of traditional Christian images with the insights of various contemporary and new age approaches to the spiritual life. In the process, I am endeavoring to chart the first steps of a path that will enable future explorers and adventurers at the edges to revitalize the traditional Christian images, on the one hand, and, on the other hand, provide a stable foundation for novel images of faith, life, death, and health.

In the spirit of Whitehead's own "organic" philosophy, each chapter is symbiotically related to all the others. Our quest for meaningful death, our desire for health and healing, our commitment to spiritual discipline, and our hope for eternal life are not isolated from one another. Our insights and discoveries in any of these areas open up unexpected questions, adventures, and insights in every other facet of our lives. It is my hope that this book will provide the signposts for the journey we must take, so that our journey will be one of anticipation, adventure, and hope.

When the servant fled toward Samarra, his journey was one of fear and hopelessness. He knew about death, but his knowledge overwhelmed him. His journey was one of dread rather than adventure, for he had no vision, ritual, or symbol to mediate hope and healing in the midst of his flight. His only response was to seek to control his fate through avoidance. As Christians, we, too, must come face to face with the inevitability of death, not in the spirit of control, but in creative openness to death and the Spirit that renews life at its edges.

Notes

[1]Robert Jay Lifton and Eric Olson, *Living and Dying* (New York: Bantam, 1974), p. 15f.

[2]*Ibid.*, p. 9.

[3]*Ibid.*, p. 16.

[4]Nelle Morton, *The Journey Is Home* (Boston: Beacon Press, 1986).

[5]Throughout this essay I will seek to respond to the insights of the "new age" movement. I view this movement both positively and critically. Yet, I realize that defining the new age movement or movements is almost an impossibility. The strength as well as the weakness of the new age movement has been its grassroots and noninstitutional character. Although the new age embraces movements and practices as diverse as *The Course on Miracles*, Unity, psychic channeling and spirit guides, rebirthing, crystals, and tarot cards, the common focus of all these practices is the belief in the power of the mind and spirit in personal transformation and health. In contrast to the modern worldview and to mainline Christianity, which has often allowed the modern worldview to set its agenda, the new age is characterized by a profound belief that the spirit is not only real but is the primary reality in the universe. Transformation occurs when we waken from our dream of separation and sin and discover the god within ourselves and all things. Often eclectic, the new age embraces Eastern religions and Christian gnosticism, white magic and acupuncture. Despite the tendency of many new agers to make uncritical claims for their techniques, the new age, like the charismatic movement, has become a spiritual home for many persons who are dissatisfied with the sterility, lifelessness, and modesty of mainstream religion.

Perhaps the best overall works on the spiritual as well as cultural implications of the new age are Marilyn Ferguson's *The Aquarian Conspiracy* (Los Angeles: J.P. Tarcher, 1980) and Fritjof Capra's *The Turning Point* (New York: Bantam, 1983). Journals such as *Common Boundary* and *New Realities* examine and integrate the many streams of "new age" thought and practice with the wider cultural milieu.

[6]For those interested in further study of the work of Alfred North Whitehead, I suggest the following works: *Science and the Modern World* (New York: Macmillan, 1925); *Religion in the Making* (New York: Macmillan, 1926); *Process and Reality* (New York: Macmillan, 1929 [Corrected Edition: New York: Free Press, 1978]); *The Function of Reason* (Princeton: Princeton University Press, 1929); *Adventures of Ideas* (New York: Macmillan, 1933); and *Modes of Thought* (New York: Macmillan, 1938).

[7]Whitehead, *The Function of Reason*, p. 8.

2

From Despair
to
Transformation

The Loneliness of the Dying

"In the midst of life, we are surrounded by death."
(Martin Luther)

Whether or not we are aware of it, each moment's arising and perishing presents us with many experiences of death and loss. Long before we face our own deaths, we experience the reality of death through the loss of relationships, the death of friends, the aging process, and the many forms of symbolic death that threaten our sense of meaning and self-affirmation. We die as we live, and our response to the deathful moments of everyday life partly determines our response to the finality of our own personal death.

One of the most compelling accounts of the contemporary response to death in its many forms is Leo Tolstoy's *The Death of Ivan Ilych*. Though it was written more than one hundred years ago,this work portrays in frightening and stark detail the denial of death and the consequent denial of life so common-place in our time. Ivan Ilych's life and death, wrote Tolstoy, is "the most simple and most ordinary and therefore the most terrible."[1] Although he is a successful magistrate and the envy of his social circle, Ivan Ilych lives a life of emptiness and superficiality. His duty and personal goals are defined by his social position and the expectations of his peers. Although he is not in love, he marries because marriage is expected of persons in his social situation. Though his marriage soon becomes boring and unsatisfying, he responds to its deathfulness by plunging himself all the more into his career. Despite his spiritual bankruptcy, Ivan believes he is living an exemplary life—indeed, from his perspective, his "life continued to flow as he considered it should do—pleasantly and properly."[2] In his career as well as in his marriage, Ivan Ilych excludes everything fresh and vital. He lives in three worlds, whose edges seldom meet: his unsatisfying marriage and family life, his upwardly mobile career, and his after-hours recreation. In describing the overall quality of Ilych's life, Tolstoy ironically repeats words reminiscent of a litany: "So they lived, and all went well, without change, and life flowed pleasantly."[3] Does this sound familiar? How many times does this scenario occur in our narcissistic, upwardly mobile society? The illusion of control and compartmentalization characterize the deathful life.

As one might expect, beneath the facade of his pleasant and unreflective life, Ivan is dying both spiritually and physically. Without warning, at a time when he reaches the apex of his career, the first signs of terminal illness manifest themselves. At first, quite subtly, Ivan Ilych experiences a strange taste in his mouth and an uncharacteristic irritability at the smallest of things. The quiet yet incessant pain in his side reveals that something is wrong. In the midst of life comes an illness from which there will be no recovery. And so begins Ilych's confrontation with his own mortality, a possibility he had neither desired nor prepared for. He has no resources to face the challenges of life. The social milieu that has been Ivan Ilych's authority and guide provides him with no direction, for neither the mores of social propriety nor the pathway of upward mobility sees the preparation for death as relevant to personal success.

As he faces his own mortality, Ilych is alone and lonely. Despite his "pleasant" life, he has neither experienced nor sought intimacy. Neither his wife nor his bridge partners nor his legal associates really know him, nor do they care to be his companions on the dark journey ahead. To all appearances life goes on as usual for Ivan and his family, in spite of his growing weakness and sense of alienation. The continuing normalcy of his family life is a charade, which they know only too well how to enact. Ivan and his wife neither speak of their hopes nor share their fears. There are no tears. There is no expressed anger. There is no expression of love. His illness seems merely to be a nuisance, complicating their otherwise "agreeable," yet deathful, life as a family. In the courtroom Ivan hopes to banish death as well: "I will take up my duties—after all I lived by them."[4] And we would add, "I will die by them!" In the midst of his most clever attempts to avoid the reality he fears to name, the specter of death presents itself. There is no escape from the gnawing pain in his stomach and from the despair he seeks to repress.

> Ivan Ilych would turn his attention to it and try to drive the thought of it away, but without success. It would come and stand before him and look at him, and he would be petrified and the light would die out in his eyes, and he would begin asking himself whether It alone was true.[5]

Even his subtlest attempts to hide from the truth could not shield from him the one reality that most terrifies and consumes him: his own imminent death. For those who have lived on the surface, who have never tested their depths or traveled to the edges of their known world, death is always surprising and tragic in its inevitability. There is no adventure—only hopelessness, fear and denial.

The hopelessness of Ivan's physical state is mirrored in the disease that has crippled his spirit. When for the first time Ivan turns inward, he discovers to his horror only an empty and lifeless self. He sees his pleasant and well-ordered life for what it is: a sham. He discovers how far he has drifted from the vital springs of joy and self-awareness. In a brief moment of self-confession, Ivan reflects: "it is as if I had been going downhill while I imagined I had been going up. And that is really what it was. I was going up in public opinion, but to the same extent life was ebbing away from me. And now it is all done and there is only death."[6] Yet, the very admission that his life had been a sham is so frightening that initially he dismisses it from consciousness.

In his final days, Ivan's agony is spiritual rather than physical. The burden of denial, hopelessness, and self-justification leaves him exhausted and panic-stricken. Yet, in the midst of his denial, a voice from within continues to torment him: "What if my whole life has really been wrong?"[7] Whereas previous generations saw death as an opportunity for spiritual growth and generativity, Ilych suffers passively in both his living and his dying.[8]

Is there any hope for Ivan Ilych? Is there any hope for us as we face the emptiness and despair that confront us at the edges of life? How do we name the sinfulness of this void and, even more importantly, how can we name and claim redemption in such a context? If Christian faith and its symbols have any meaning for human life, they must address the edges of experience where life and death meet—where death can be *lively* or life can be *deathful.*

These are key phrases that recur throughout this book. A deathful or "death-filled" life is a life whose vitality is sapped by a denial of the interplay of life and death. By contrast, a lively death is animated by an embrace of the totality of one's experience of life and death. A lively death, ironically, finds its vitality precisely in an embrace of that which is normally feared or repressed. As we repress our experiences of death, we also deaden our experience of life.

The plight of Ivan Ilych represents well the current shape of sin in our society, which Christopher Lasch describes as "narcissistic."[9] What can our faith and our tradition of theological reflection say to the person whose inward journey reveals only emptiness and whose outward prognosis represents only the mystery of the unknown?

In the past few years, the books of Scott Peck have found their way to the reading lists of Christian laypeople and clergy alike. There is a quantum leap between the optimism of his earlier book, *The Road Less Traveled,* and the stark realism of his later book, *The People of the Lie.* The latter book convicts a generation of self-centered, outwardly striving, and emotionally empty "baby-boomers" and their parents of being people who lie not only to themselves but to others, and who wreak havoc by their self-deception.[10] The lie is the denial of the self in its totality. "Evil is that which kills the spirit" and deadens the vitality of life.[11] Beneath a veneer of goodness, Ivan Ilych and a whole generation are victims of the lie because they cannot face the emptiness and ambiguity at the depths of their existence. The Christian community has yet to address the everpresent self-deception that leaves emptiness at the center and terror at the edges of life. I seek to respond to this critique by providing Christian laypersons and clergy a foundational theology of living and dying, based on the insights of the study of death (thanatology), psychology, and theology.

Visions of Transformation

From thanatology: Elisabeth Kübler-Ross and Stephen Levine

The thanatology movement owes its current vitality and impact on society to the courage and creativity of Dr. Elisabeth Kübler-Ross. From her initial seminars with dying patients in 1965 to her current concern with the needs of persons dealing with AIDS, Kübler-Ross has been the leading voice for transformation of our cultural attitudes toward death and dying. Her work embraces both the personal and the institutional aspects of the study of death. At the heart of her work is the affirmation that the confrontation with death is the source of life's meaning and generativity. Kübler-Ross believes that the experience of dying "does not have to be a catastrophic, destructive thing; indeed, it can be viewed as one of the most constructive, positive, and creative elements of life."[12] Although Kübler-Ross's critics have accused her of romanticizing death, the wisdom of her "stages of dying"—the experiences of denial, anger, bargaining, depression, and acceptance—is found in her recognition that the ultimate goal of acceptance is not achieved through "positive thinking" alone, but through the willingness to embrace and accept the totality of one's life. Affirming the experience of death is necessary for a truly holistic approach to life.

Kübler-Ross challenges us to affirm creatively the reality of death. Apart from such affirmation and support, the dying process remains a time of repression, meaninglessness, and, sometimes, regression, rather than an opportunity for growth and transformation.

Our culture's alienation from death and from dying is revealed not only in its ostracism of dying persons but also in the denial and paralysis surrounding the AIDS epidemic. Kübler-Ross invites us to view AIDS as the "ultimate challenge," whose threat challenges us to go beyond repression and alienation from death to transformation and concern for life. Indeed, our response to AIDS involves much more than being informed on issues of medicine and lifestyle. Our response to the AIDS epidemic has implications for our very survival on the planet. It "is our choice to grow and learn from it, to either help the people with this dread disease or abandon them. It is our choice to live up to this ultimate challenge or to perish."[13]

Although Kübler-Ross does not claim to be a philosopher or a theologian, her work goes far beyond the medical response to death and dying. She believes personal self-actualization and social well-being relate directly to issues of human destiny. In the concluding paragraphs of *Death: The Final Stage of Growth*, Kübler-Ross consolingly writes:

> There is no need to fear death. It is not the end of the physical body that should worry us....Death is the final stage of growth in this life. There is no total death. Only the body dies. The self or spirit, or whatever you may wish to label it, is eternal.[14]

Our encounter with death opens us to life and love and, therefore, to the possibility of the evolution of humankind toward its ultimate destiny.[15] Our lives and our deaths participate in the broad scope of personal and spiritual evolution. In a "spacious" universe in which our spiritual journeys involve countless lives, Kübler-Ross wonders if somewhere beneath the pain and despair of the AIDS crisis, there is a hidden force inviting us toward greater spiritual evolution. Kübler-Ross raises the intriguing question, "Is it possible that our AIDS patients, children and adults alike, chose to contribute their short life spans on planet earth to help us open our eyes, to raise our consciousness, to open our hearts and minds, and to finally see the light?"[16] Without romanticizing the role of persons with AIDS or accepting Kübler-Ross's belief in reincarnation, it is clear that there is much we can learn from their adventures at the edges of life.

As Kübler-Ross suggests, hope for the dying person is to be found in the experience of self-awareness and self-acceptance, and in the insight that our deaths are part of the larger process of personal and planetary evolution. There is hope even for an Ivan Ilych: as Ivan, his family, and physicians face their own mortality and despair, they may experience the unexpected intimacy and life-full transformation that their death-full life has blocked. Death is "the final stage of growth" for those whose courage and vulnerability opens them to the potential for adventure and transformation residing within their fear and pain.

Stephen Levine is perhaps the most respected thanatologist within the "new age" community. A colleague and friend of Elisabeth Kübler-Ross, Levine responds to the needs of dying persons and their families through a creative and eclectic synthesis of Buddhist, Hindu, Jewish, and Christian wisdom. Levine believes that the exploration of death is the primary catalyst for spiritual awakening.[17] Whether actual or symbolic, the confrontation with death reminds us that we are all terminal. Indeed, there are but two kinds of people: those who are aware of the dying process within them and those who are unconscious of it. As I face the prospect of my own death, the primary question is "Who dies?" The initial answer is "I do!" And, yet, we find ourselves wondering whether there is a deeper reality, beneath our sense of separation, which is universal and undying. We hope the answer is "yes."

Levine suggests that much of the pain associated with death results from our attachment to our static and inflexible ideas of ourselves and our roles in life. The consequence of such attachment is the repression of all that reveals the illusions associated with that belief that we can control and manage our world. Suffering arises from our refusal to acknowledge and accept the totality of our experience, including the deathfulness of our lives. "Our suffering is caused by holding on to how things might have been, could have been, should have been."[18] As I reflect on my own life, I ask myself, "Who am I? What would be left over if sickness forced me to let go of my accustomed roles and images of myself? What if I could not be a minister or professor? What if I could no longer earn an income or have eyes to read or the strength to play catch with my son? Who would I be?" Like Ivan Ilych, I try to banish such thoughts from my mind. Yet, to experience wholeness and peace, even at the edges of life, we must deny nothing, including the reality that our lives, like all things, are ultimately insecure and everchanging.

Levine proposes that the ultimate illusion is death. Although death appears to threaten the rigid and isolated ego, it cannot touch the true spiritual self. "Death or the process of dying seems to be accompanied by a sense of expanding beyond oneself, of dissolving out of form, of melting into the undifferentiated."[19] Levine calls us to live consciously and to die consciously. We are challenged to let go of the notion of a limited and independent self. In so doing, we become open to the whole of life and move from *our* pain to *the* pain of the universe, from *our* joy to *the* joy of the universe. As Christians, we would have to add: from *our* salvation to *the* salvation of the universe in the love of God. Released from the bondage of the ego, "we experience the superficiality of the self we have clung to for so long. As we see the nature of this dreamlike separateness, we recognize there is, in reality, no one to die and that it is only the illusion of this separate someoneness that takes birth again and again."[20] For Levine, we are deathless, because we are ultimately selfless.

The hope for the dying person, according to Levine, is found in selfless self-acceptance. The moment of awakening comes through our nonjudgmental openness to the totality of life. In the moment of awakening and letting go, we discover that beyond the self we have so desperately clung to is the Self which unites all things. Stephen Levine invites us to reflect upon a new image of the self, one whose inclusiveness and relationality embraces both life and death. This deeper Self is for us, as Christians, not merely the impersonal self of the universe, but the personal Spirit of God, who unites all things and bears witness within our own spirit by its constant prayer within our own prayers (Romans 8:15, 26–27).

From psychology: Ernest Becker and Robert Jay Lifton

Although images from religion and thanatology abound in the works of Ernest Becker and Robert Jay Lifton, both root themselves in the classical tradition of psychology. Whereas Kübler-Ross and Levine emphasize the role of death in self-transformation and personal discovery, Ernest Becker vividly paints the shadow side of mortality in his classic work, *The Denial of Death*. Despite the everpresent reality of death, our main task and central calling in human life is heroism.[21] Indeed, for Becker, the primary purpose of society is to encourage heroism and personal meaning by proclaiming the significance of everyday, commonplace existence.[22] Yet, the urge to be heroic, to stand out, and to leave a mark is constantly threatened by the transitoriness of all human achievements. The pyramids, the Roman Empire, the United States, and even my own church will all pass away. Consequently, beneath the facade of everyday life and its stability lies our basic terror in the face of death.[23]

Becker believes that culture and religion exist, ultimately, to repress or lessen the basic anxiety that arises from the realization that, in spite of our spirituality, reason, and imagination, we are earthly and mortal.[24] To face reality as it is is to plunge oneself into an experience of terror. Becker maintains that we must repress the reality of death, at least partially, in order to commit ourselves to tasks whose impact is only temporary and ultimately insignificant in the wider scope of reality. Some form of repression, or forgetfulness of our true situation in life, is necessary if we are to experience inner value and personal security.[25] Yet it is a well-known psychological fact that the process of repression blocks our awareness of the heights and depths of life. Becker contends that because the world is both too wonderful and too terrible for us to experience directly, we unconsciously create the illusions of culture and religion to filter reality and help us cope. Yet, when these illusions break down and we discover the deathful nature of life, we are left with two options: mental illness or authentic heroism.

In Becker's world, where the unconscious fear of death lies beneath every human project, authentic health be can found neither in the exercises of mental adjustment nor in the projections of positive imaging. In the spirit of the existentialist philosopher Søren Kierkegaard, Becker maintains that authentic health and full humanity come from facing the terror of "nonbeing" and experiencing fully and creatively the anxiety of one's mortality. "Full humanness means full fear and trembling at least some of the working day."[26] In a world where our primary strategy is often to avoid anxiety, self-acceptance does not mean peace but openness to the terror of life. The anxious confrontation with the ultimate deathfulness of life is the foundation of true heroism. Becker's hero is like a "knight of faith," totally within the world, yet trusting what lies beyond it, as he or she battles the dragons found at the edges of life.[27] Psychic well-being is grounded in "a lived, compelling illusion [or metaphor for reality], that does not lie about life, death, and reality."[28] We cannot stare into the sun indefinitely; we cannot live indefinitely without "illusion." If religion is to encourage psychological health at life's edges, Becker believes it must balance our anxiety in the face of death with our ultimate trust in life's meaning.

Becker maintains that a person has "to stand on his [or her] own feet, to face up to the eternal contradictions of the real world."[29] Or, as Whitehead puts it, "Philosophy may not neglect the multifariousness of the world—the fairies dance and Christ is nailed to the Cross."[30] Accordingly, Becker views Eastern religion—and, quite possibly, the optimism of new age philosophies—as evasions of reality, "fused with a sense of magical omnipotence...a manic defense and denial of creatureliness."[31] We cannot evade mortality, anxiety, and doubt. The darkness is as real as the light.

In contrast to the images of growth and self-actualization heralded by Levine and Kübler-Ross, Becker confronts us with the possibility that death is still basically tragic, and hope an illusion. Becker leaves us at Good Friday, with no promise that Easter will follow. Ironically, the disillusionment, central to Becker's realism, is a creative factor in human growth. The breaking down of our illusions allows us to experience life "as it is" in both its raw wonder and its raw terror.

Christianity and Judaism have always understood that religious symbols are relative, finite, and, at some level—to use Becker's terminology—"creative illusions." Yet, contrary to the critiques of Becker, the very vitality of religious symbols in shaping human experience and our own personal experiences of unexpected healing and growth point to the existence of a divine reality beyond our metaphors and images. Beneath the terror of life and death, there is a force whose presence promises ultimate healing even at the edges of life.

Robert Jay Lifton is noted for his work on the interplay of death and transformation. Arising from his studies of Hiroshima survivors, Vietnam veterans, and, more recently, the psychological effects of the nuclear arms race, Lifton has recognized the significance of images of death and immortality in the formation of human experience. Lifton's work revolves around the insight that "to live in the face of death, man [sic] requires a sense that his life has continuity and significance."[32] For Lifton, the primary question raised by the everpresent reality of death is: "How can a person live without overwhelming anxiety in the face of death?"[33] For Lifton, the dislocating experience of death drives us to discover and create images of "symbolic immortality," or connection, beyond our own individual lives.

The presence of such images in the formation of the self and its social environment enables persons and societies to affirm the meaning and significance of life without denying the inevitability of death. Whereas Becker sees the concept of immortality as a denial of death, Lifton proclaims that the concept of symbolic immortality is "our best avenue toward acceptance of death and confronting our own finiteness."[34] In the spirit of the psychologist Carl Jung, Lifton sees the existence of symbols as being central to our interaction with the world. Accordingly, the various images of immortality are not just "creative illusions" or psychic constructs; they give life and structure to our experience.

For Lifton, our basic need is to experience meaning and historical connection in the face of death. In the context of the everpresent threats of death and alienation, an affirmation of symbolic immortality provides the vehicle through which a person experiences the sense of a context, reflecting the "relatedness to all that comes before him and all that follows him."[35] Apart from such culturally accepted and personally integrated symbols of immortality, we are "numbed" and are unable either to face death or to affirm life. Lifton believes that the last half of the twentieth century is a time in which we have lost our sense of connection both with history and with nature. Facing global destruction, the ambiguity of technology, and the unfamiliarity of death, without any access to compelling and vital images of immortality and connection, has left many persons rootless and alienated not only from their own experience but from the cosmos as a whole.

Traditionally, we have faced death and dislocation through the affirmation of one or more of the following images of symbolic immortality: the biological (immortality in terms of one's offspring and the continuity of one's family and social grouping); the creative (immortality in terms of the impact of one's work and vocation on the future); the theological (the conquest of death through eternal life); the natural (immortality in terms of one's participation in the natural world); or experiential transcendence (the experience of immortality arising from the "mystical" transformation of everyday experience). Lifton believes that the general erosion of the experience of symbolic immortality in each of these areas of life has led to "psychic numbing" and the inability of persons to commit themselves to values beyond their personal interest. For Lifton, the personal and the social experience of death are essentially related. We cannot fully understand the meaning of our personal deaths. As a culture we deny the reality of death in war by the computer graphics that describe the deaths of thousands of soldiers and civilians in Kuwait and Iraq as if they were part of a fantasy video game. The strength of Lifton's view is his recognition that the creative confrontation with death pertains not only to that particular dying person as he or she faces mortality, but also to the psychic health of the community from which the individual comes. Lifton believes that our very survival depends on our willingness "to open ourselves to the experience of pain and to the imagery and anxiety of death."[36] Therefore, we must commit ourselves to personal and social transformation if our civilization is to survive, find new meaning, and revive its spirit of adventure.

Lifton sees the symbolic images of the "survivor" and the "protean" (constantly changing) self as particularly powerful in our time. "The survivor is one for whom having known the end makes possible a new beginning—a beginning freshly unencumbered by the weight of the old and the dead."[37] The "survivor," similar to Becker's hero, embodies the natural images of "death and rebirth." In the midst of touching death in some real or imagined way, the survivor discovers the resources that will enable her or him to embrace both her or his own personal existence and social environment in a new way. While others are numbed to the realities of death and destruction, the survivor dares to explore and experiment with the dark edges of existence. She hears the cries of the poor and feels the death of the rain forest as part of her own living and dying.

As a psychic adventurer, the survivor embraces the "protean quest" for new and unexpected images of self, family, society, and God. Like Becker's "hero," the "protean" adventurer finds inspiration to dream and to experiment, to embrace the familiar as well as the foreign, and to venture forth with no clear destination and few instruments, other than one's own experience, for navigation. There is always the possibility of self-disintegration. Nevertheless, Lifton believes that the protean adventure is itself a source of integrity and insight. To find its destination, the protean self must strive to "remain constant in every metamorphosis," that is, to maintain "the struggle for coherence and the integration of the self, in the midst of the shape-shifting process."[38] In moments of personal insight, the protean adventurer glimpses a wider horizon of psychic space and time that enables her or him to find direction for the next step of the journey.

Lifton's work is pioneering in its recognition of the deep

connection between the personal and the social dimensions of death and immortality. Lifton's emphasis on the interplay of images of death and immortality in personal experience invites the adventurer to be creative in the formation of her or his vision of reality. Lifton expresses the conviction that in the midst of confronting the possibility of our own deaths or the death of the planet, we will discover those images of rebirth that aid in the transformation of ourselves and our culture's death-denying institutions.

what I am doing —

Lifton and Becker challenge persons of faith to become adventurers in our own spheres of influence. The God we worship is also an adventurer, who calls us to be companions on a journey from the wilderness to a land of abundance. We cannot fully control either the destination or the path to it. It is likely that there will be darkness and pain along the way. Yet, like countless faithful adventurers who have preceded us, we travel trusting that within and beneath all that threatens us, we are connected with one another and with a Presence whose guidance and companionship are trustworthy.

From theology: Paul Tillich and Teilhard de Chardin

The task of theology is to reflect on the presence and meaning of God in human experience. Although the theologian often utilizes the insights of psychology, philosophy, and thanatology in her reflections on mortality, the reality of death compels theologians such as Paul Tillich and Pierre Teilhard de Chardin to explore the edges of life in terms of the divine-human relationship. Christian theology must address the dark side of human experience, if it is to be faithful to the message of the cross.

Paul Tillich (1886–1965), the German-born theologian who spent much of his professional career teaching at seminaries and graduate schools in the United States, described his personal and academic life as being "on the boundary." Although Tillich's work is highly technical, it is also an expression of his own personal pilgrimage, his own attempt to live courageously amid the constant threat of meaninglessness, anxiety, and death.

Tillich saw the confrontation with death as the primary issue of our faith. Within every life lived, we experience the "shock of non-being," the recognition of the fragility of our lives.[39] This awareness of our finitude and vulnerability finds expression in the everpresent, but often repressed, experience of anxiety. Although we seek to domesticate our basic anxiety by relating it to specific, controllable objects of fear, such as losing a job or failing a test, beneath every specific experience of fear is the basic anxiety of nonexistence, which we can neither control nor predict.[40] We are anxious because unconsciously we realize that, in spite of our quest for security through relationships, insurance policies, job promotions, and military expenditures, there is no real security within our world. In the context of this "shock of non-being," we may either constrict our lives by the avoidance of death (the way of neurosis), or embrace our vulnerability and affirm ourselves in spite of all that threatens us (the way of courage).[41]

Tillich maintains that self-affirmation in the face of the threat of "non-being" in all its forms (death, guilt, meaninglessness) is found in the experience of a power that embraces every threat.[42] Religion is, accordingly, the state of being grasped by the power of God, or Being itself.[43] Here faith and courage intersect. Authentic courage is found in faithful trust and self-affirmation even when the presence of God seems absent. With Jesus we cry out, "My God, my God, why have you forsaken me?" Yet, our protest of God's absence is testimony to our faith that God is somehow present. In our despair and disillusionment with ourselves and the gods of our own creation, there is a power that enables us to be courageous and whole. When we would despair that God has abandoned us in times of need, we are reminded that the solitary set of "footprints on the sand" represent those moments when God has anonymously carried us.

Tillich, like Becker, provides a path for those whose illusions have been shattered and whose gods have died. Our experiences of brokenness and despair point beyond themselves to the reality of Being-itself, the unknown but living God whose presence overcomes every threat.[44] Yet God is more than a cosmic principle. Being-itself cannot be our companion, lover, and friend. Tillich's image of God is far too impersonal to address the needs of persons at the edges of life. When the foundations of our lives have crumbled, we need a God who is fully personal, who cares about us, who shares our sorrow and responds to our pain. We need a God who shares our own adventure and walks beside us as we journey toward our own Calvary. This image of an intensely personal and relational God must not be a figment of our imaginations or a projection of our desires. Rather, our image of God must reflect our deepest intuitions of reality not only as we experience it in our own lives but as we see it revealed in the historical witness of scripture and the testimony of the church throughout the ages. Here, as we shall see, the process-relational thought of Whitehead and his followers provides the image of a lively God, whose loving presence embraces even the edges of life.

Pierre Teilhard de Chardin (1881–1955) was one of the most creative theological synthesizers of recent times. Throughout his life, Teilhard sought to be both a scientist and a Christian. A priest in the Society of Jesus, the Jesuits, Teilhard spent much of his professional life studying fossils and seeking to find a synthesis between evolution and Christian faith. Whereas many persons see science and faith as antagonistic to each other, Teilhard believed that the ultimate source of the evolutionary process is God's spiritual presence deep within the world of matter. The universe in its evolutionary journey is aiming toward its goal, the Omega Point, the ultimate spiritualization of all things in Christ.

In the context of Teilhard's optimistic spirituality of evolution, it is surprising to read Henri de Lubac's assessment that all of Teilhard's thought, even his scientific work, is one long meditation on death.[45] But if the spirit of God is present as the force of evolution in all things, it must also be present as the power of transformation in our own experiences of aging, infirmity, and death. Teilhard maintained that death serves a purpose in the physical evolution of species, for without death, the earth would be stifling and growth would be stunted.[46] Yet, death is also the greatest physical and moral evil we face. Teilhard asserts that death in all its dimensions can be overcome only "by finding God in it."[47] When death is seen as part of God's ultimate purpose, then death becomes the primary agent of transformation. By opening us through the experience of vulnerability, God makes room for God's own presence to penetrate and fill our deepest selves. Though we are called to be agents of growth and opponents of suffering, we are also called to seek unity with God in the midst of suffering. Teilhard's prayer is for God to "teach me to treat my death as an act of communion."[48] As Christians face our own crosses, we are called to identify with the redemptive suffering of Jesus. "The Christian is not asked to swoon in the shadow, but climb in the light, of the Cross."[49]

Teilhard's reflections on death reveal the paradox found in the Christian attitude toward death. On the one hand, we are to oppose death in all its guises as an evil to be defeated. But on the other hand, we are called to accept death as an essential element of spiritual transformation. Nevertheless, we must ask, where do we find God in death? How do our lives make a difference to God and the spiritual evolution of the planet?

Concluding reflections

The common insight of theology, psychology, and thanatology is that there *is* hope for the lost and dying person, for the person whose illusions have been shattered by the reality of death and personal brokenness. Despite their different perspectives, the thanatologists, psychologists, and theologians we have considered agree that through the confrontation and acceptance of our deaths, we can experience profound growth and unexpected spiritual transformation. The possibility of transformation is grounded in the courageous affirmation of the totality of life, even at its edges. This is very different from "positive imaging" and "positive thinking." As "twelve step" and other recovery programs have maintained, the "good news" of transformation occurs only when the "bad news" of one's personal situation has been admitted. When a person experiences "hitting rock bottom" and, for the first time, sees himself or herself without illusion, the process of transformation begins. When I realize that "I'm not OK, and you're not OK, but that's OK," the edges of life become pathways to healing.

In the remainder of this chapter as well as the next, we will explore the contribution of Whitehead's philosophy and process-relational theology to the creative encounter with mortality—first in terms of its understanding of human existence and its social environment, and then in terms of the presence of God at the edges of life. Process-relational theology, as it is seen in the work of John B. Cobb, David Griffin, Marjorie Suchocki, and others, understands God, the world, and Christian experience primarily in terms of dynamic change and social relatedness. In utilizing the insights of Whitehead and the process theologians influenced by him, I will seek to provide an answer to death that embraces and builds upon the insights of scripture, thanatology, psychology, theology, and new age thought. As I reflect upon my own experience of death and loss, I believe that process thought encourages us to make sense of the reality of death and the life-giving presence of God at the edges of life.

Death and Human Existence

Metaphysics and meaning

Whether or not we call ourselves philosophers, we all live by an implicit metaphysical vision. A person's metaphysical vision is basically her interpretation or understanding of the world in which she lives. Some of us live by a very personal, and usually unconscious, metaphysical vision that not only organizes our world but also shapes our response to the persons and events we encounter. Early in life, we may have discovered that the world is not trustworthy and that our needs and feelings are unimportant to those around us. We learn not to expect much of ourselves or our world. Because the world we perceive is un-trustworthy, we are always on our guard and fearful of the future. Yet, there are times when we ask ourselves, "Is this understanding of reality the whole story? Is this the only possible way of interpreting the world in which I live?"

Our metaphysical vision shapes not only what we experience but also what we deem possible for ourselves and others. What would the world look like if we viewed it as an essentially good but occasionally ambivalent environment that, nevertheless, is supportive of our highest aspirations?

From the philosopher's point of view, metaphysics seeks to be more than just the study of our own personal interpretations of reality. Rather, the metaphysical quest is to discover those elements of reality that characterize all our experiences at their deepest level; that is, it seeks to unearth those basic realities that all creatures share, despite their unique interpretations of reality. As the history of philosophy and theology reveals, there are many possible interpretations of what is most important and most characteristic of the reality we experience.

The courage, creativity, and adventure we seek at the edges of our lives cannot be achieved in a "cosmic" vacuum. Human existence requires the recognition of a cosmic background within which the human project finds meaning and continuity. Metaphysics eventually intersects with our personal quest for meaning. Our interpretation of reality not only reveals what is important to us but also provides us with guidelines for our living and our dying. To interpret the world as essentially meaningless and godless, as many materialist philosophers do, is to provide few resources for persons at the edges of life. To deny the reality of the spiritual world is to interpret the experiences of mystics, healers, and common persons drawn to prayer in times of crisis as, at best, foolish illusions and, at worst, lies. Accordingly, it is important to reflect on our personal as well as cultural metaphysics. While all metaphysical visions are finite and fallible, an outmoded or incorrect interpretation of reality can be a matter of life and death, especially if it prevents us from experiencing resources for healing and spiritual transformation.

Process-relational thought suggests another way of seeing the world. From the vantage point of process thought, the world is a lively, dynamic, meaningful, and forward-moving community. Humanity is not alone in a meaningless world, nor is humanity the center of the universe. God shares in the same lively and dynamic world of relationships that supports ourselves. Spirituality is not an illusion nor is healing an impossibility. Both are basic to reality. In a world of process, the edges of life are fluid and a lively death is always possible.

In the chapters ahead, we will explore the significance of process-relational thought for persons seeking health and wholeness in painful and seemingly hopeless situations. In so doing, we will discover a theological as well as personal foundation for courage, creativity, and adventure at the edges of life.

The dynamics of human existence

Our reflection on death began with the words, "in the midst of life, we are surrounded by death." From the very first moments of philosophical and religious reflection, authentic human existence has always been connected with the preparation for death. For Christians, death is perceived both as the greatest evil and as the primary gateway to the experience of salvation. Indeed, the reality of death implicitly conditions every moment of life. From our first breaths, our individual lives are constituted by a series of "mini" deaths. We venture forth from the safety of our parents' arms to take our first stumbling steps. We say "goodbye" to the security and comfort of our homes to enter the frightening, yet freeing, world of the university. We bid farewell to children as they begin a new life on their own. We let go of a career that spans four decades as we prepare for the unstructured adventure of retirement. The very nature of life is a process of "perpetual perishing," in which we are compelled by the very nature of reality to "die" to the past in order to confront the novelty of the present and the uncertainty of the future. Yet, though the experience of death is everpresent in its many forms, our most difficult project is this very process of responding to the transitory nature of life. Many of us are like the rich young ruler, who would rather cling to the security of the past, than venture forth to the new life that God promised him in the future (Matthew 19:16–22). The primary challenge of life is learning to die each day by continually letting go of the familiar past and the fleeting present.

The issue of "letting go," or detachment, is theological as well as personal. Many philosophies see stability as the primary reality. Their vision of reality claims that, in spite of the radical physical and psychological changes we undergo during our lifetimes, the deepest reality of all things is unchanging and stable in nature. Change is often viewed with suspicion and fear, whether it relates to religious truths, social practices, or personal opinions. Stability and changeless perfection are sought after at any cost. But this view of reality makes the experience of change and relationship a problem and, in the lives of persons and institutions, leads either to clinging to the status quo or the concept of the "self" as it is imagined to be, or to viewing personal and social changes as essentially threatening in nature. In recent Christian history, the "fundamentalist" attempt to preserve a prescientific understanding of the world and human experience is an obvious example of this fear of change and growth.

Process-relational thought, on the other hand, affirms the dynamic and relational nature of reality and human existence. The dynamic and fluid nature of reality applies even to our own personal experience.

If we reflect on our experience at this moment, we will discover that it is best described in terms of process and change. From moment to moment, our experience, like an ever-flowing stream, is in constant flux as countless thoughts, memories, feelings, and sensations arise only to be replaced by new and different thoughts, memories, feelings, and sensations. Personal identity cannot be found in stability, for no absolute stability is to be found. Even the body, whose permanence seems undeniable, is in constant flux; its apparent stability disguises the liveliness of organs and cells that are constantly dying and being replenished.

Even that which we call our "self" is really a stream of experiences, each of which is intimately related to the others by a common past and a projected future.[50] In order to understand the stream of interrelated experiences characteristic of personal existence, it is essential that we first investigate the most basic element of reality, the actual occasion. Whether we speak of the self in this moment's experience, the nature of God, or the characteristics of molecules comprising a cell in the lymphatic system, "actual occasions," according to Whitehead, are "the final real things of which the world is made up."[51] Although actual occasions differ in complexity of experience and importance for their environment, these "complex, and interdependent drops of experience" are the building blocks of all things.[52]

Every "drop of experience" is social in nature. It is a process of feeling the universe from its own momentary perspective. What we call the self, or the momentary center of our experience, emerges with its experience of the world, arising out of the data it feels. Accordingly, no actual entity stands apart from the flow of life. Our experience at any given moment is influenced implicitly by every element in the universe. As I sit at my computer on this cold December day, I am affected not only by the intensity of students studying for finals at the university library, the glare of the computer screen, the feeling of my fingers on the keyboard, and the tolling of the nearby clock tower, but also by the movements of planets and constellations, the political developments in Eastern Europe and in the Middle East, by repressed childhood memories of death, success, and failure, and by the recent memory of my mother's death. Beneath it all, I experience my own intention to spend the afternoon working on this manuscript. All these elements, and many more, constitute my momentary experience of my "self" and my momentary organization of the "drops of life" that are mine to experience in the flow of life going on around and within me.

Long before the ecological movement became a factor in public consciousness, Whitehead recognized that everything that exists is constituted by its relationships. The cosmos constantly witnesses to the reality of the "Butterfly Effect," the recognition that in some small way everything influences everything else, that a monarch butterfly moving its wings in Los Angeles has an impact on the wind currents in Washington, D.C.[53] Social relationships are neither accidental nor an afterthought; they are basic to reality. There are no brute and isolated facts just as there can be no truly independent, self-made individuals.

In the flow of relationships, each drop of experience arises from the past, which limits its possibilities and shapes its experience. But the heaviness of the past combines with the impact of our immediate and "cosmic" environment to provide the basis for unique experiences of intensity and beauty to emerge. At this very moment, your conscious experience is a synthesis of bodily inheritance, visual stimuli, thoughts and feelings, not to mention the causal influences of your past and of the wider political and global environment. Because of this, in this very moment, the extent of your freedom is quite limited. Conformity to the past is a "cosmic" as well as personal reality. Yet, the fact of your choice to shape the next momentary drop of experience in a particular way is also a "cosmic" and personal reality. In each moment you are also making choices that shape the present and condition the future not only for yourself but for the whole universe. Freedom is a personal as well as cosmic reality.

My own conscious or unconscious aims—for example, the desire to complete this paragraph before my next appointment as well as the desire to play basketball with my son this afternoon—shape how I experience my immediate environment, and whether I experience the knock on my door as a nuisance or as a welcome diversion. Perhaps I write or think faster, or the opposite may occur, in relation to my anticipated activities, depending on how I let them motivate me. My very act of self-creation contributes something novel to the universe, even if my book is never published and no one but myself reads the paragraphs I am writing at this moment.

Each drop of experience is an expression of novelty, or new life, resulting from its own inner goal toward intensity of experience in the immediate present and in the relevant future.[54] No one feels the universe, or even the same event, exactly the way I do, nor does anyone experience the universe from the same personal and physical perspective that I do.[55] Both cosmically and personally, we are never fully conditioned by the past nor are we ever passive victims of our upbringing, past behavior, or medical condition. We are free, though limited in that freedom, even if only in terms of our response to what we experience.

We recognize this element of freedom whenever we choose to affirm life and the possibility of growth in spite of illness, personal failure, or spiritual distress. Even in the midst of the horror and inhumanity of the German concentration camps, Jewish psychologist Victor Frankl and evangelical author Corrie ten Boom embraced, and yet transcended, the evil they experienced by choosing to affirm the small portion of freedom they did possess. Faced with the irrationality of death on a daily basis, they, nevertheless, chose to live by a vision of reality that was larger than the evil of the concentration camp—to complete an important work in psychology and be worthy of the love of one's family (Frankl), or to be faithful to God (ten Boom), enabled them to face their suffering courageously and faithfully.[56]

Every drop of experience arises from its inheritance and transformation of the universe it experiences. However, in every moment it must also die to the immediacy of the recent past and the present in order to give birth to the world that succeeds it. There is always the temptation to hold onto the comfort and security of the past, even when the past has been painful and constricting. Yet, as Jesus proclaimed, "those who find their life will lose it, and those who lose their life for my sake will find it" (Matthew 10:39). Like Abraham and Sarah, we are challenged to leave behind the familiar in order to receive the unseen promise of new life.

Although an occasion of experience is momentary and fleeting, its influence endures beyond itself as a contributing factor in the formation of the universe. This interrelatedness of the past, present, and future is described by Whitehead in terms of "objective immortality." The drops of life that we call ourselves "perish subjectively, but are immortal objectively."[57] Each moment of experience perishes and yet lives on as a factor in the emergence of its successors. Although its successors, including the next momentary "self," experience the actuality and feeling tones of the past as their own, they must conform to what they experience. More simply put, in its own immediacy, each drop of experience inherits the gifts of its predecessors, synthesizes their contributions in its own moment of experience, and contributes its unique value to the future both of its own stream of experiences and of the ongoingness of the universe in God. Nothing of value is ever lost. Everything makes a difference to God.

Such metaphysical reflection leads to questions of value, self-understanding, and faith. Whitehead's metaphysics of experience and social relatedness provides a basic framework for responding to the "many" (and the "mini") deaths of each day as well as to the finality of my own personal death. First, Whitehead's metaphysics reminds us that life itself is a process of perpetual perishing. Death and rebirth constitute the very nature of reality from which there is no escape. The attempt to cling to the past or the present goes against the dynamic process of the universe and is the primary source of anguish and disappointment. To be attuned to the nature of things means to open oneself to the grief of every moment's death as well as the surprise of every moment's birthing. This is the process of life, and it includes death.

Even as we welcome the freshness of the new moment, we are reminded that in order to embrace the new, we must let go of the past and consign even the most vital experiences to memory. The recognition of death and loss in life is necessary for moving toward openness and rebirth. The price of clinging to the past is, therefore, not just stagnation, but movement toward further death—the natural and healthy flow is toward life in all its abundance.

The emergence of each new moment from the womb of life is a call to an adventure into unknown and uncharted territories. Harmony with the universe and God's movement within it requires our breaking free of the past and welcoming the often unsettling call of the future. Saul died to the secure legalism of his religious upbringing and was reborn and given a new name, Paul, as he faced the freedom and uncertainty of God's grace. We die to the image of youthful omnipotence to be reborn as wise and generative adults. Even a serious illness or the loss of a job may invite us to explore new dimensions of ourselves at the edges of our lives. In my own life, a crisis in my marriage and the death of my image of my wife and myself compelled me to discover new sources of security and new ways of relating, which enabled our relationship to grow even amid the tension and struggles. The recognition of the perpetual perishing of all things is a call not only to embrace the experience of the "many" (and "mini") deaths but to anticipate and prepare for the death that will bring a culmination to the series of moments I and others call my self.

The second significant contribution of Whitehead's metaphysics to an understanding of death is its emphasis on the presence of creativity in every situation. Self-creation involves not only the acceptance of what is and what cannot be changed but also the recognition that we are not absolutely determined by the past or the present. Although we cannot change the data of our experience, we can, in one brief moment of self-creation, determine how we will experience and shape that "data" forever. Our responsibility is not so much for what happens to us but how we respond to the "brute" facts of existence. My mother's recent death can be an occasion for denial and unhealthy guilt, or it can also be an opportunity for thankfulness, appreciation, and sensitivity to those who grieve. Accordingly, the urge toward novelty challenges the inherent tendency as well as temptation to conform, repeat, or become attached to the past. The world is neither entropic nor caught in the grip of original sin. The God who is always doing a new thing constantly urges us to venture forward even at the edges of our lives.

In a world in which existence implies creativity, there are no absolute "dead ends" for the living. We are not prisoners of our illness or our pain. Although our life-situations may radically limit our freedom in some areas, within the matrix of our unique life situation lie unexpected possibilities for growth and transformation. Within these possibilities, death can become an experience of wholeness and completion rather than brokenness and loss.

Robert Jay Lifton asserts that we require a sense of continuity between the past, present, and future in order to affirm the meaning of our lives in the context of death. Whitehead's doctrine of "objective immortality" responds directly to the need for our momentary experiences to have everlasting significance. The ongoing process of life always entails the loss of the immediacy of the present moment. In a world of independent and isolated substances, what is lost can never be recovered. In such a world, authentic connection is impossible since my relationship to the world never fully touches myself, nor does my own life essentially shape the life of another. Process thought, in  contrast, maintains that our actions truly make a difference in the experiences of others just as our body's well-being shapes our conscious experience. We are all part of a "body," where each experience enters into and becomes embodied in the lives of all the others. We are internalized and immortalized by the presence of our lives in other drops of experience. I say this not abstractly but very concretely in terms of my own personal experience of living in accordance with this principle of connectedness. This principle makes it possible for prayer and affirmations to change lives and world events. My prayers do not end with my own consciousness of another person's need but radiate across the universe and shape, at least on an unconscious level, the experience of the one for whom I am praying.

Connection and compassion are metaphysical realities with deep moral and personal implications. Compassion means to "feel with," or share fully, the experience of another. In a world of dynamic relationships, compassion is not an option. We cannot avoid sharing in the feelings of others. Nor can we avoid sharing our own, even unconscious and disguised, feelings with others. Each moment of experience is endowed by the gift of its predecessors. In its own perishing, each moment's self-creation is a gift that conditions future occasions by providing the data from which its successors emerge. Our intentions as well as our actions, our feelings as well as our words, ripple across the environment. With confidence that our lives make a difference in the temporal world, we can have faith in the face of death that our lives truly matter to persons known and unknown and that our compassion and aspirations will not be lost. In connection and compassion, all drops of experience flow creatively into each other and into that which we Christians call "eternity." Life and death are transcended and "love never ends" (1 Corinthians 13:8).

From denial to transformation

In spite of the connectedness affirmed by Whitehead's doctrine of "objective immortality," our own personal deaths mark the end of the world as we have known it. Life goes on and is enriched by each individual's contribution. But each physical life ends. Apart from the hope of survival after death, each person assumes that he or she will have no further adventures. Before this abyss of personal nonbeing, the only authentic feeling is our experience of anxiety. For some with strong beliefs in life after death, this anxiety will be wedded with hopeful anticipation of unknown adventures that lie ahead. For most of us, the anxiety is the primary reality.

You may think I am asking too much of my readers to suggest that you try to integrate this basic anxiety of death and the grief of "perpetual perishing" with the transforming freshness of "adventure." But I suggest that the healing and creativity we seek at the edges of life is ultimately the gift of a metaphysical, or theological, vision that allows us to affirm life in its totality. This is surely at the heart of the apostle Paul's faith that, in spite of all the threats that confront us, "Nothing can separate us from the love of God" (Romans 8:39). Life affirmed in its totality does not need to be pulled apart at its edges. The flow of life can continue right into the unknown and unexpected. It actually does each day. Just hours after I reassure my mother that nothing will go wrong with her operation, the phone rings and I hear the news that there is little hope she will survive the night. I am shocked and overwhelmed as I face her imminent death. I want to deny her death, but the emptiness and grief I feel during the long plane ride back to California assures me of its reality.

How do we respond creatively to the death of a loved one? How can we live adventurously when we've just discovered that we ourselves are at the edges of life?

Building on the affirmation of life in its totality, Whitehead describes three responses that organisms make to stressful changes in their environment. Although Whitehead's analysis of challenge and response pertains to all life events, it is particularly relevant to our personal and cultural encounter with death. Each response to death reflects a particular interpretation of reality and attitude toward life.

(1) The primary response organisms make to any threat to their existence is the blocking out of unwelcome detail.[58] This response occurs on a primitive biological level as well as on a more complex and sophisticated level. In our experience, we call this response "denial." By following the way of denial, the path usually taken by stable and noncreative organisms, an organism survives by acting as if the threat either does not exist or has no significance. When a healthy young woman receives the diagnosis of leukemia, her first response may be, "It can't be true, I'm a runner, I eat right, I don't smoke—there must be some kind of mistake."

In her description of the stages of dying, Kübler-Ross points out that denial may play a positive as well as a negative role in a person's response to the diagnosis of a life-threatening illness. According to Kübler-Ross:

> Denial may be a healthy way of dealing with the uncomfortable and painful situation with which some of these patients have to live for a long time. Denial functions as a buffer after unexpected shocking news, allows the patient to collect himself and, with time, mobilize other, less radical defenses.[59]

Yet if denial is maintained indefinitely, it eventually leads to isolation and the inhibition of personal growth.

Repressing the recognition of one's own mortality, or the threat of global ecological collapse, through explicit denial, frenzied activity, or excessive consumption may initially produce the appearance of serenity. But the blocking out of unwelcome details, described by Whitehead in terms of "anesthesia," is ultimately bought with the price of a deadened spirit and the haunting uneasiness that beneath the veneer of normalcy lies the turbulence of unresolved anger, grief, and fear. As Ivan Ilych discovered, despite his attempts to go on with life as usual, the reality of death always surfaced. The illusion of normalcy cannot be maintained indefinitely. Eventually it will collapse, leaving one unprepared for the rush of feelings and images of mortality that accompany one's actual life situation.

While this reality remains a widely accepted psychological fact, for Whitehead it also has an important metaphysical reality as well. What we place in the background of experience always leaves its mark. Every exclusion of reality, especially that which is psychologically denied and repressed, leaves its "scar" in terms of an emotional feeling (for example, fear, panic, or anger) that blocks or diverts one's total flow of experience. Constant denial leads, as Lifton and Whitehead point out, to the inability to feel or respond to one's authentic experience at all. It leads to deathful life, to entropy, repetition, and boredom. The very process of denial saps energy and creativity from persons and projects alike and leaves in its wake a vague uneasiness at the edges of consciousness that can be neither identified nor eliminated.

The blocking out of unwelcome detail eventually blinds one both to the possibilities of the moment and to the lure of the future, and eventually robs one of the vitality born from embracing the whole range of bodily and inner feelings that constitute one's experience. Indeed, since the primary characteristic of living organisms is novelty, the path of denial eventually leads to a deadness of spirit that mirrors the course of one's own illness.

(2) Whereas the "blocking out of unwelcome detail" anesthetizes the spirit into believing that the threat of death does not exist and that change and transformation are unwarranted, a second, equally destructive response to life-threatening news is described by Whitehead as "acute disruption."[60] The experience of acute or chaotic disruption occurs when the threat of death, or any significant environmental or personal change, leaves one

so overwhelmed that no other possibilities are recognized except those of destruction. The threat of death can so dislocate our sense of self that we lose our own personal center. Death and death alone, or the frantic flight from death, can become the center around which we shape our interpretation of reality. When he could no longer evade the reality of his condition, Ivan Ilych began to wonder "whether It [death] alone was true."[61] Ilych "would go to his study, lie down, and again be alone with It: face to face with It. And nothing could be done with It except to look at It and shudder."[62]

This is "acute disruption." In the experience of this radical upheaval, the reality of the present moment and the terror of the future can leave us totally shattered. The possibility of death effectively ends the possibility of living, for we perceive ourselves as too weak to face reality. In facing life-threatening illness, institutions, patients, and family members are often so shattered by the possibility of death that they perceive the dying person as already dead. The future holds nothing but silence, sedation, and television. Growth under such conditions is viewed as impossible. Novelty and transformation are alien and illusory hopes, occurring only beyond the grave. There is nothing more to do but wait. The shattered self must be anesthetized until unwelcome death occurs. Ironically, the stark awareness of death characteristic of chaotic disruption often leads to denial and the construction of a stable, unfeeling, and rigid self whose central project is to isolate and protect itself from the threat of novelty.

Although the psychological experience of anesthesia and acute disruption appear different, each is symptomatic of the inability to face the anxiety of nonbeing. In the face of death, both imply that there can be neither growth nor wholeness, and both responses bring about this reality. Again, this has its metaphysical as well as psychological reality. Both see the self as isolated, weak, and bereft of external support. Whereas denial deadens the spirit through stagnation, acute disruption can lead to the disintegration of the self through rootless frenzy. In both cases, the self is isolated and disconnected from the nurturing and compassionate realities of our community and the wider cosmic environment. Death becomes the savage and unmerciful "god," whose presence renders us helpless and hopeless. In our terror and paralysis, we are unable to release ourselves from our bondage and pain—to let go of our own meager security, to embrace the pain and terror, and to allow life as well as death to flow through ourselves. Only hopeless waiting remains for the person and the institution that bows down, helpless and passive, before the god of death. Despite the appearance of so-called "vital signs," the person has already died both spiritually and energetically. The popular maxim "get a life" becomes sadly appropriate for many persons trapped by this plight.

(3) While all persons at the edges of life experience some forms of denial and chaotic disruption, Whitehead offers a more positive response to the threat of "nonbeing." This is the way of adventure and "creative transformation." It is a sharp contrast to passivity and victimization. The experience of creative transformation is, first of all, grounded in acceptance, which opens us to the healing possibilities available in each moment. Acceptance is both a personal and a metaphysical response to life. To commit oneself to the ongoing process of acceptance is to affirm life as it is—to recognize the transitoriness and vulnerability as well as the connectedness, compassion, and novelty of life. It is to discover within our "perpetual perishing" and mortality a deep sense of stability and connectedness rooted in the interplay of the past, present, and future. Acceptance enables one to let go of the illusion of the unchanging, invulnerable and isolated self, in order to embrace the self as it is—dependent, relational, protean, and resourceful.

Acceptance arises from the metaphysical insight that the negativity of grief and suffering result, in part, from a false interpretation of reality. The debilitating pain of life arises precisely from our denial of the most basic elements of experience—connectedness and interdependence on the one hand, and perpetual perishing and transition on the other. Pain and grief, then, are most appropriately interpreted not as life-denying evils but as essential to the experience of life itself. As Stephen Levine points out, "We wish we were otherwise and that is our hell, our resistance to life....To be whole we must deny nothing."[63] To experience our pain and grief as it is, without denial, is to discover that even amid the brokenness we experience, the edges of our lives flow into a deeper reality. To lose the rigid and narrowly defined self is to find the Self permeating all things, the Living God.

In those moments of shock when the imminent death of my mother became a reality, I felt emotionally torn. I wanted to hide from my pain and run away from the reality of her death. Yet I could not control my tears and anguish. Out of the depths of my own pain, all I could do was cry and utter words of grief and words of faith. But in the starkness of my pain and dislocation I also felt a sense of holiness that I seldom experience in everyday life. The truth of our experience, even our pain, can, as scripture proclaims, "set us free."

To accept the totality of life we must affirm what *is*, and thus let go of our old perceptions of ourselves and the universe. Acceptance is not passive submission to deterioration and death. Nor is it a stark realism that abandons all hope. The affirmation of the totality of our lives does not exclude the experience of anxiety, self-doubt, and fear. In confronting the abyss of personal nonbeing, bodily as well psychic chaos may threaten the very integrity and centeredness of the self. One may well discover the demonic as well as the angelic in oneself. Against such possibilities, one may be tempted to embrace the monotony of deathful life rather than the adventure of lively death. Only by going beyond and through the chaos and discord can we encounter the possibility of transformation. Only then can we integrate our psychic and physical threats into a more comprehensive unity. In this unity, even dissonance and despair become elements contributory to the experience of "courageous self-affirmation."

Whitehead would say that in directly embracing the threat, the occasion of experience "originates novelty to match the novelty of the environment."[64] In so doing, the "unwelcome detail" (for example, the diagnosis of cancer) is placed within a more inclusive perspective, in which it is but one of the factors defining one's experience and sense of self.

Acceptance requires a painful realism. For example, someone might admit, "I have cancer and I may die. I feel afraid. It hurts to think that I may become weak and dependent. I'll miss seeing my son grow up." Yet, with this radical acceptance comes the equally radical recognition that death is not the only possibility that confronts one in the present moment. Someone might also admit her life situation, but see it in the context of life-affirming personal and metaphysical affirmations. She might affirm, "I have cancer. I may die. But today I am alive. I will experience as deeply as possible the love I have for myself and the love others have for me. I will share my love, for love endures forever. I am open to God, whatever happens to me."

The anxiety felt at facing the reality of one's medical diagnosis does not encompass the totality of one's existence. Although acceptance and self-affirmation do not initially alter the data or prognosis of the illness, they transform one's perception of one's illness and enhance the possibility of a meaningful future. A young man, whose complications from AIDS led to a diagnosis of lymphoma, affirmed to me following a series of chemotherapy treatments, "I have AIDS and lymphoma but neither AIDS nor lymphoma controls my life. I am going to live my life fully in whatever time I have left."

As we will see in chapter four, the path of acceptance and creative transformation is at the heart of O. Carl Simonton's approach to the treatment of cancer. In his analysis of personal responses to the diagnosis of cancer, O. Carl Simonton suggests that when some persons receive the diagnosis of cancer, they give up; they cannot cope with the reality of the illness; they see no future and no possibility for change. There is only waiting for death to occur. In contrast, others refuse to become "cancer patients," or persons defined solely by their disease. Such persons experience their cancer from a new perspective as they envisage their cancer cells as weak and confused compared to the power of their own inner resources and the medical care they are receiving. To the creative spirit, radiation and chemotherapy are more than treatments with drastic side effects. They are celebrations of life and healing. Through their renewed sense of meaning and self-affirmation, some are even healed. Yet, even for those who die, the process of dying becomes a generative experience—a testimony to the connectedness and immortality of all things. As one cancer patient proclaimed:

> Now I can be in a room with a hundred people and know I am no less alive than the healthiest person there. My mind tells me: "As long as I am not dead, I am alive. Fully alive." No longer do I feel as I did before, that I am slowly dying, watching myself die, half alive, half dead. Now, for me, receiving chemotherapy is a moment of living. Hurting like hell is a moment of living. Being frantic with loneliness is living, living, living. Naturally moments of joy and pleasure are moments of living— everyone knows that—but I am learning not to differentiate so much.[65]

As his own life ebbed away, Ivan Ilych's physical sufferings were terrible, but "worse than the physical sufferings were the mental sufferings, which were his chief torture."[66] He could face neither his death nor the possibility that his well-ordered life had been a sham. As Tolstoy notes, "he tried to defend all those things to himself and suddenly felt the weakness of what he was defending. There was nothing to defend."[67] The past as objective fact could neither be changed nor nullified. Ivan's life, like so many others, had been a "huge deception which had hidden both life and death."[68] Yet in the midst of his despair Ivan began to perceive his life from a new perspective. As he fell into the abyss of darkness he discovered an unexpected light. In its presence, he no longer needed to justify himself. Although he could not undo the past, he could transform its meaning for himself and his family through forgiveness. Though his final words were inarticulate and masked by his agonizing screams, Ilych's spirit was at peace. In his moment of dying, Ivan "sought his accustomed fear of death and did not find it. 'Where is it? What death?' There was no fear because there was no death."[69] In place of death, Ivan Ilych discovered light, safety, and the reality of redemption.

Notes

[1]Leo Tolstoy, *The Death of Ivan Ilych and Other Stories* (New York: New American Library, 1960), p. 104.

[2]*Ibid.*, p. 112.

[3]*Ibid.*, p. 119.

[4]*Ibid.*, p. 132.

[5]*Ibid.*, p. 133.

[6]*Ibid.*, p. 148.

[7]*Ibid.*, p. 152.

[8]Philippe Aries, *Western Attitudes Toward Death* (Baltimore: Johns Hopkins Press, 1974), p. 11f.

[9]Christopher Lasch, *The Culture of Narcissism* (New York: W.W. Norton and Company, 1979).

[10]M. Scott Peck, *The People of the Lie* (New York: Simon and Schuster, 1983), p. 75.

[11]*Ibid.*, p. 42.

[12]Elisabeth Kübler-Ross, editor, *Death: The Final Stage of Growth* (Englewood Cliffs: Prentice-Hall, 1975), p. 2.

[13]Elisabeth Kübler-Ross, *AIDS: The Ultimate Challenge* (New York: Macmillan, 1987), p. 13.

[14]Kübler-Ross, *Death: The Final Stage of Growth*, pp. 164, 166.

[15]*Ibid.*, p. 165.

[16]Kübler-Ross, *AIDS: The Ultimate Challenge*, p. 12.
[17]Stephen Levine, *Meetings at the Edge* (New York: Doubleday, 1984), p. x.
[18]Stephen Levine, *Who Dies?* (New York: Doubleday, 1984), p. 3.
[19]*Ibid.*, p. 270.
[20]*Ibid.*, p. 253.
[21]Ernest Becker, *The Denial of Death* (New York: Free Press, 1973), p. 1.
[22]*Ibid.*, p. 7.
[23]*Ibid.*, p. 11.
[24]*Ibid.*, pp. 20, 26.
[25]*Ibid.*, p. 53.
[26]*Ibid.*, p. 59.
[27]*Ibid.*, p. 258.
[28]*Ibid.*, p. 204.
[29]*Ibid.*, p. 279.
[30]Alfred North Whitehead, *Process and Reality* (New York: Free Press, 1978), p. 338.
[31]Becker, *The Denial of Death*, p. 280.
[32]Lifton and Olson, *Living and Dying*, p. 9.
[33]*Ibid.*, p. 53.
[34]Robert Jay Lifton, *The Future of Immortality* (New York: Basic Books, p. 1987), p. 16.
[35]Lifton and Olson, *Living and Dying*, p. 60.
[36]*Ibid.*, p. 114.
[37]*Ibid.*, p. 122.
[38]Lifton, *The Future of Immortality*, p. 18.
[39]Paul Tillich, *Systematic Theology* (Chicago: University of Chicago Press, 1967), Volume One, p. 198.
[40]Paul Tillich, *The Courage to Be* (New Haven: Yale University Press, 1952), p. 38.
[41]*Ibid.*, p. 66.
[42]*Ibid.*, p. 155.
[43]*Ibid.*, p. 156.
[44]*Ibid.*, p. 180.
[45]Henri de Lubac, *Teilhard de Chardin: The Man and His Meaning* (New York: Mentor-Omega Books, 1965), p. 108.
[46]*Ibid.*
[47]Pierre Teilhard de Chardin, *The Divine Milieu* (New York: Harper Torchbooks, 1957), p. 82.
[48]*Ibid.*, p. 90.
[49]*Ibid.*, p. 104.
[50]Alfred North Whitehead, *Modes of Thought* (New York: Free Press, 1968), p. 163.
[51]Whitehead, *Process and Reality*, p. 18.
[52]*Ibid.*, p. 18.
[53]James Gleick, *Chaos: Making a New Science* (New York: Penguin, 1987), pp. 11-31.
[54]*Ibid.*, p. 27.
[55]*Ibid.*, p. 85.

[56]Victor Frankl, *Man's Search for Meaning* (New York: Simon and Schuster, 1964).

Corrie ten Boom, *The Hiding Place* (Washington Depot, Connecticut: Chosen Books, 1971).

[57]*Ibid.*, p. 29.

[58]Whitehead, *Process and Reality*, p. 101.

[59]Elisabeth Kübler-Ross, *On Death and Dying* (New York: The Macmillan Company, 1969), p. 39.

[60]Alfred North Whitehead, *Adventures in Ideas* (New York: Free Press, 1967), p. 259f.

[61]Tolstoy, *The Death of Ivan Ilych*, p. 133.

[62]*Ibid.*, p. 134.

[63]Stephen Levine, *Who Dies?*, p. 10f.

[64]Whitehead, *Process and Reality*, p. 102.

[65]Stephen Levine, *Meetings at the Edge* (New York: Anchor Books, 1984), p. 22f.

[66]Tolstoy, *The Death of Ivan Ilych*, p. 152.

[67]*Ibid.*

[68]*Ibid.*

[69]*Ibid.*, p. 155.

3

The Dying-Rising God

Death and the Question of God

The quest for courage and adventure at the edges of life leads us to the frontiers of religious experience, to questions of "ultimate concern" and "ultimate reality." As Paul Tillich maintains, the courage necessary for self-affirmation in the face of death and ultimate meaninglessness finds its answer in the God who remains when the finite gods of our own creation have failed. Although to some degree the ultimate reality is always mysterious and unfathomable, I believe that the spiritual quest requires each of us to envisage images of God arising from our own particular understanding of human existence and its cosmic environment. This is especially important in a time in which the traditional images of immortality and divinity are questionable to many persons, even in the church. In the search for creative images of the divine, our theological reflections must affirm that God is present both within and yet beyond all human imaging. In fact, the affirmation of God's "omnipresence"—that is, God's presence everywhere and in all things—implies that the world and, indeed, human experience in all its aspects reveals God's nature. Accordingly, our understanding of God reveals something, however relative and partial, both about ourselves and ultimate reality itself.

We become like the objects of our worship and trust. The images upon which we focus shape our lives, and are reflected in our values, our ethical decision making, and our responses to issues of vocation and the meaning in our lives. Our understanding of the character and activity of God determines our response to matters of life and death as they relate to ourselves, the persons we love, and the institutions that simultaneously reflect and condition our lives. Therefore, I would invite you, the reader, to consider those images of God that are most powerful in your life. Which images enliven your spirit? Which images would deaden your spirit, should you begin to find yourself conforming to them?

As we seek to live creatively and adventurously at the edges of life, the question of God becomes crucial. New life requires openness both to our own resources and to resources beyond ourselves. In Christian experience, God is the ultimate source of comfort, security, and adventure. But our images of God have often robbed life of its zest, and left persons at the edges of life feeling lonely and abandoned. At life's edges, adventure and creativity require the image of a god who is our faithful companion and friend, a god who redemptively embraces death as well as life. I believe that the image of God articulated in Whitehead's metaphysics and in process theology enables us to face death directly, while affirming the importance of our lives in the present moment. But first, let us explore the impact of traditional images of God on persons at life's edges.

Divine Comfort at the Edges of Life

One of the primary roles of religious life is to provide comfort and hope to the dying and the grieving. At the edges of life the believer is reminded that as she is dying, she is nevertheless in God's hands. To the person near death, *The Book of Common Prayer* of the Episcopal Church gives these words of assurance: "Almighty God, look on this your servant, lying in great weakness, and comfort him with the promise of life everlasting, given in the resurrection of your Son Jesus Christ our Lord. Amen."[1]

The litany at the time of death concludes with these words of promise for those who mourn:

> Into your hands, O merciful Savior, we commend your servant. Acknowledge, we beseech you, a sheep of your own fold, a lamb of your own flock, a sinner of your own redeeming. Receive him into the arms of your mercy, into the blessed rest of everlasting peace, and into the glorious company of the saints in light. Amen.[2]

The words of liturgies for the dying proclaim the trustworthiness of God in all things. To those whose death is imminent, God is proclaimed as "our refuge and strength, a very present help in trouble" (Psalm 46:1). The dying are reminded that nothing "in all creation will be able to separate us from the love of God in Christ Jesus our Lord" (Romans 8:39).

Past and present liturgies within the Christian tradition orient dying and grieving persons toward God as the ultimate source of salvation and comfort. In the Middle Ages, the "arts of dying" sought to awaken persons at the hour of death to the realities of judgment, eternal life, and divine faithfulness. The awareness of death was essential in the drama of living and dying: the hour of death was the moment of decision between the divine and the demonic. Even today, the rituals and language of faith inspire the awareness both of human mortality and divine immortality. We do not live or die on our own, or even by our own power. Our living and dying occur in the presence of God, who is the Alpha and the Omega, the beginning and the end of all things. In its burial liturgy, *The Book of Common Prayer* affirms that God alone is the source of human hope:

> Thou only art immortal, the creator and maker of mankind; and we are mortal, formed of the earth, and unto the earth shall we return. For so thus thou didst ordain when thou created me, saying, "Dust thou art, and unto dust shalt thou return." All we go down to the dust; yet even at the grave we make our song: Alleluia, alleluia, alleluia.[3]

Beneath the comfort and assurance provided by the traditional images of God has stood an image of God that has been theologically as well as morally ambiguous. God is the center of religious experience, but heart and mind have been at odds in the understanding of God's relationship to the world. On the one hand, Christians have affirmed that God's love embraces all creation, including sinful and dying humanity. God hears our prayers and is present within our own spiritual struggles. On the other hand, God has been envisaged by theologians and clergy as essentially distant, aloof, unchanging, and coercive in relationship to humankind, a judging king rather than a loving parent. In piety and printed word, theologians and laypersons have proclaimed a God who comforts and heals the afflicted. But the reigning metaphysical images of God have withheld from God's nature the very qualities that make authentic love and comfort possible.

In contrast to the classical tradition of theology, my vision of God, arising from the insights of process thought, is one in which heart and mind are reunited, in which our affirmations regarding God's relationship to us reflect our personal experience of God's love as both steadfast and surprising. My vision of God is rooted in the lively, dynamic, and relational God of the biblical tradition. God is not coercive but gently persuasive, much like the pastor at the bedside of the dying, and this persuasion to grasp life even at its edges, even amidst death, comes from a "metaphysics of love" in which images of sin, evil, and judgment have no ultimate place.

The Tension Within the Traditional:
The Classical Conception of God

To justify such an apparent "quantum leap" in conceptualizing God, let me first retrace the origins of the classical conception of God in contrast with the image of God I affirm. Our great tradition of classical theism is grounded in the interplay of Greek metaphysics and biblical theology. This integration of Greek and Hebrew thought is both the strength and the weakness of classical theology and its metaphysics. At the heart of the classical vision is the attempt to integrate love, perfection, and power within the divine unity. In the spirit of the scriptures, the classical tradition affirms that the love of God is revealed in three primary ways: the creation of the world, the incarnation of Christ, and the redemption of humankind. God's love is active and self-giving. The life and death of Jesus Christ reveals the depths of God's love for sinful and undeserving humankind. The universality of God's love is further demonstrated by God's willingness to reach out to the ungodly and the lost, without consideration of merit or lifestyle. Accordingly, God's love is outgoing, active, creative, and redemptive in nature. These affirmations about the nature of God have been the foundation for the creeds as well as the piety of Christians throughout the ages.

This vision of a loving God was seriously undermined by the church's adoption of the Greek idea of perfection as the primary characteristic of God's nature. From the Greek perspective, perfection is related to both changelessness and independence. The church was left with the paradox of maintaining that God was both loving and yet essentially unrelated to the world. In his analysis of classical theism, Charles Hartshorne makes the scathing comment that "it is worthy of note that the religion which more than all others held that God cares about his creatures tried to adopt a philosophy which, logically carried out, implied that God is literally and rigorously indifferent to the world."[4] If divine perfection means changelessness, then God is aloof, inflexible, and therefore indifferent to the world.

At the heart of the classical notion of perfection lies the belief that God is eternal and unchanging. Change of any kind would imply a metaphysical and moral "deficiency" in the divine nature. How can God be good if God witnesses the actions of evil people? How can God be perfect if God experiences pain and suffering? How can God be changeless if God responds to particular human needs? From this perspective, only a changeless God can warrant our worship and trust. A God who suffers loss or lack cannot be depended upon to rescue us from the afflictions of life, nor can a suffering God be trusted to ensure our ultimate salvation. From the perspective of classical theism, a dynamically changing and passionate God, who is truly touched by the world, is "too much like ourselves" to be worthy of worship. Divine holiness requires that God not only be "wholly other" but literally "the same yesterday, today, and tomorrow."

The classical image of God's changeless perfection owes its origin, in good measure, to the integration of Hebraic monotheism with Aristotle's concept of the "Unmoved Mover." The ultimate source of cosmic movement, Aristotle affirms, must be itself "eternal, a substance and an actuality," a universal object of desire that moves without itself being moved.[5] The divine must exist in a state of changeless self-contemplation, for "He is thinking of that which is most divine and most honorable, and He is not changing; for change would be for the worse, and this change would then be a motion."[6] In this classical view, although God moves all things by the very beauty of God's nature, God neither knows nor needs the world. God's supreme blessedness is found in the divine self-contemplation, undisturbed by the imperfection and the transitoriness of the world. The person who most embodies the divine nature needs neither society nor friendship—he is the truly "self-made man," a fully independent substance wrought in the image of the divine substance.

The distance between this model and contemporary images of the healthy person is obvious. It is even further removed from the biblical image of Jesus Christ. Today, we understand mental health and spiritual well-being in terms of growth, sensitivity, and compassion, whether it is expressed toward our children, our neighbors, or a stranger. Indeed, aloof indifference to the "cries of the poor" and the "groaning of creation" is a manifestation of sin rather than of spirituality. Two thousand years ago, the incarnation of God in the world was understood in terms of suffering, companionship, and love. The "friend of sinners" was hardly aloof or distant from the imperfections of life.

When Christianity adopted Aristotle as its philosopher, it subordinated the passion of divine love and the relational quality of the incarnation to the Greek image of metaphysical perfection. Although God embraces and permeates all things, God is neither changed nor influenced by this relationship to the world. The classical understanding of God's relationship to the world is totally asymmetrical: out of God's fullness, God creates a world that God cannot really know. The world in its emptiness can give nothing to its creator, for God needs nothing. Could any child flourish with such a parent? Yet this is the dark side of the classical notion of God's "fatherhood." We need God but God does not need us.

Such a world does not even "have a prayer." Although our prayers and piety may benefit us and may contribute to the growth of human community, they cannot be heard by this impassive and immobile God. As clearly as any theologian before or since, the eleventh-century theologian Anselm expressed the tension between God's love and God's perfection characteristic of classical theology:

> For, if thou art passionless, thou dost not feel sympathy; and if thou dost not feel sympathy, thy heart is not wretched from sympathy for the wretched; but this it is

to be compassionate. But if thou art not compassionate, whence cometh so great consolation to the wretched? How, then, art thou compassionate and not compassionate, O Lord, unless because Thou art compassionate in terms of our experience, and not compassionate in terms of thy being.

Truly, thou art so in terms of our experience, but thou art not so in terms of thine own. For, when thou beholdest us in our wretchedness, we experience the effect of compassion, but thou dost not experience the feeling. Therefore, thou art both compassionate, because thou dost save the wretched, and spare those who sin against thee; and not compassionate, because Thou art affected by no sympathy for wretchedness.[7]

Classically speaking, prayer is a purely private and personal act. It means nothing to God. It only consoles ourselves and those for whom we pray. In addition, this vision of God devalues the world in which we live. A world that cannot directly enter into and condition the divine experience is ultimately meaningless and valueless in itself.

Even articulate and well-intentioned expositions of the traditional image of God, such as Swedish theologian Anders Nygren's *Agape and Eros*, cannot overcome the contradiction between changeless perfection and passionate love. In the spirit of the classical tradition, Nygren affirms that God's love (*agape*) flows toward sinful humanity without regard to distinction, and creates value in an otherwise useless object. As Nygren maintains, "God does not love what is already in itself worthy, but on the contrary, that which has no worth acquires worth just by becoming the object of God's love."[8] Yet, although Nygren correctly recognizes that divine grace is indifferent to the distinctions of righteous and sinful, God's grace, in order to be relevant and redemptive, must make distinctions. Grace does not come to humankind in general but to persons at particular moments in their lives. Further, the classical image of God degenerates into "narcissism" if the object of love derives its only value from being loved. In the final analysis, a divinity that experiences no value as a result of its relationship with the world is as diabolical and destructive as a parent who cannot see the value of its child apart from its parental caretaking. An isolated deity, who acts but cannot hear, provides no redemptive image of hope for persons facing death. Just as grace comes to persons at particular moments of their lives, so God's love must be uniquely personal and flexible as it responds to the needs of persons at the edges of life.

Although the classical image of divine perfection seeks to protect the uniqueness and transcendence of God, it ultimately renders God irrelevant to the world. A world whose existence makes no essential difference to God, a world ultimately valueless apart from God's "unmotivated" love, eventually becomes a world that neither needs nor requires God for its explanation or its self-actualization. Contrary to the aims of classical theism, the vision of such a perfectly unchanging God eventuates in a liberalism that sees prayer merely as a form of communal affirmation and consolation. My experience of prayer and meditation tells me it is more than this. In recent decades, the vision of aloof and changeless perfection culminated in a Christian atheism that rightly proclaimed that both the word and reality of God are "dead" in terms of their value and significance to the "modern" world. The image of a stark, unchanging, utterly transcendent God ultimately leads to either a practical and one-dimensional atheism for humans "come of age" or a narcissistic and world-denying spirituality, created in the image of its distant and apathetic god. In either case, the God whose changeless perfection seemed the bedrock of dependability becomes the God whose aloofness leaves the suffering alone with their pain and the dying to sink into meaninglessness.

While my negative reaction to the classical perspective is not extreme, for some—who mate God's changeless perfection with unfettered power—the God of love becomes nothing less than a demonic sadist whose dispassionate power kills but cannot heal. For some, God becomes a potentate who creates pain but cannot experience it. The Augustinian-Calvinist view of God's unmerited grace for the chosen, combined with its doctrine of eternal damnation for those God has rejected, reveals the dark side of classical theism. The worship of divine power and perfection ultimately alienates humankind from the God who would seek to save it. Such images of God inspire guilt, fear, and anger, and blind us to God's everpresent forgiveness, comfort, and love.

The notion of an impassive and changeless God is the ultimate projection of our denial of death and the deathful living so destructive to human experience. Unable to feel negative feelings (or any form of authentic emotion) and anesthetized to conflict and pain in the created world, the God of classical theism provides us comfort *only* beyond the grave. There is no divine comfort in this world. An "opiate of the masses," this apathetic God promises only "rest in peace" to those who suffer chronic illness or the indignity of injustice. As the ultimate model for human good, the "God of dispassionate love" encourages its worshipers to become dependent, apathetic, isolated, and paternalistic in their love for others. Aristotle maintained that the "good person," like the God he or she admires, needs no friends. Imitating the god she worships, she gives but will not receive, she helps but will not listen *even to God.*

Despite the belief that such absoluteness is a sign of "perfection," the absolute, self-enclosed, and unchanging God is, in fact, too weak and inflexible to embrace the pain and grief of the world. Radical as it may sound, I believe that if alienation is sin, then this is truly a sinful God. Alfred North Whitehead traces the roots of this tragic and sinful abandonment of the Christian ideal of love as follows:

> The notion of God as the "unmoved mover" is derived from Aristotle, at least as far as Western thought is concerned. The notion of God as "eminently real" is a favorite doctrine of Christian theology. The combination of the two into the doctrine of an aboriginal, eminently real, transcendent creator, at whose fiat the world came into being, and whose imposed will it obeys, is the fallacy which has infused tragedy into the histories of Christianity and Mohametism.

> When the Western world accepted Christianity, Caesar conquered....The brief Galilean vision of humility flickered throughout the ages, uncertainly. In the official formulation of the religion it has assumed the trivial form of the mere attribution to the Jews that they cherished a misconception about their Messiah. But the deeper idolatry, of the fashioning of God in the image of the Egyptian, Persian, and Roman imperial rulers, was retained. The Church gave unto God the attributes which belonged exclusively to Caesar.[9]

I believe that Christianity must recover the "Galilean vision" of God if it is to respond creatively to the needs of persons in crisis and pain. We must once again see the perfection of God in terms of the life of Jesus Christ rather than the lives of earthly rulers. In Christ we glimpse a life of compassion and relationship. We see a person of deep feeling who weeps over the death of his friend Lazarus and sheds tears over the sinfulness of Jerusalem. In Jesus we see a vision of a divinity who is moved by human pain and sinfulness, who embraces our brokenness in order to heal it. In the Galilean vision of God, God is neither contaminated nor threatened by the encounter with death, pain, illness, or human sin. God's perfection is found precisely in God's redemptive compassion, or "feeling," for the lost and the hurting.

At the edges of life, the aloof, omnipotent, and majestic Caesar can neither save nor comfort. For the suffering and grieving, the Galilean vision alone can suffice. As Christians we are challenged to let go of the familiar images of omnipotence and transcendence and allow our metaphysical vision to be shaped by the image of Christ, the suffering servant and the crucified God. In his writings from the vantage point of a Nazi concentration camp, Dietrich Bonhoeffer claimed that "only a suffering God can save."[10] At the edges of life, only a "metaphysics of love," grounded in the intimacy of the Galilean vision of God, can provide us with the companionship, guidance, and support necessary for our own personal dying and rising.

The Dying-Rising God

If we are to expect divine companionship at the edges of life, envisioning a new definition of divine perfection is essential. In contrast to classical theism, the view of God developed by process-relational thought affirms that divine perfection should be defined in terms of love rather than absolute power or eternal changelessness. For human or divine love to be creative and healing, it must involve receiving as well as giving. This is the problem with the classical vision of God. God gives, but does not receive. God acts, but God's actions are unilateral. They do not take into account the needs and hopes of the world. There is another option: the envisagement of power, both divine and human, in terms of love—that is, in terms of relationship, persuasion, and sympathy.

Traditionally God has been described in parental terms, as "father" but also even as "mother." We are learning that parental love can become "paternalistic" and "narcissistic" when it onesidedly neglects the feelings and gifts of children. Healthy parental love recognizes that children are not merely extensions of their parents' desires and needs. Though the lives of children and their parents are interdependent, children have a life of their own. They have their own feelings, hopes, and desires. Authentic love recognizes and nurtures, rather than undermines, the freedom and the unique experience of children. Good parenting therefore involves empathy, imagination, freedom, and persuasion. Parents are always powerful in relation to their offspring, and their power may be used for good or for evil, for growth or for death. In this context, I believe that God's presence in the world is best perceived in terms of a persuasive, yet powerful, parental love, which receives as well as gives, and which encourages freedom as well as creativity in its offspring.

At this point, we might ask ourselves, "How is God's persuasive love experienced in our lives and in the world? Does God's existence really make a difference in our everyday lives and at the edges of life?" In response to such questions, I would suggest that John Cobb's descriptions of God's presence as the "call forward"[11] and as the "principle of creative transformation"[12] provide the best clues for discerning God's presence in our lives. God is active in the world, and God's presence makes a difference. In each moment of experience, God is present as the urge toward creativity, beauty, and transformation. At the edges of life, we experience God's "call forward" in the life of the widower who, after nearly fifty years of marriage, begins a new life on his own and affirms that new life on a daily basis by learning to cook three balanced meals each and every day. Like a healthy parent, God does not wish us to live in the past or remain dependent children. God desires that we grow in our ability to shape our lives creatively and gracefully. This is the essence of divine persuasion.

Divine persuasion, the power of God in the world, is revealed first of all in terms of God's compassion and love for each drop of experience. In order to understand the nature of God's persuasive love, we must briefly reexamine the nature of human experience. Each drop of experience arises from its "embrace" of the world. In that moment of self-creation, it shapes and transforms what it experiences into an integrated whole. As such, each moment's experience is heavily indebted to the past: past moments of pain, remembrance of failures as well as successes, habits and hopes, and bodily sensations as well as general physical health combine with the overall environment to create the contemporary moment.

The desire for adventure or new life is rare when we are first confronted with disturbing and life-threatening news. The present moment can easily be overwhelmed by the heaviness of the past or the uncertainty of the future. The cancer that consumes the flesh may also consume the spirit. Anesthesia, repression, or disintegration may become attractive options. But in such moments of dislocation we are neither alone nor are we prisoners of our greatest fears. Within our tendencies toward denial and entropy, there is another factor, which Whitehead calls the divine "initial aim." It is that impetus toward growth and wholeness that we experience alongside the feelings of disintegration and denial. God's "aim" for us is the source of hope at the edges of life.

The hope we feel is not an alien external force. It is the presence or "incarnation" of God within our own experience. As the apostle Paul proclaims, the "secret" of our hope is "simply this: Christ *in you!* Yes, Christ *in you* bringing with him the hope of all the glorious things to come" (Colossians 1:27, Phillips). God is neither beyond us nor outside of us; God is within us, seeking wholeness and redemption in this and every present moment.

At its depths, each moment of experience is grounded in its experience of God. Although the presence of God is seldom directly recognized—because we experience God indirectly in our experience of ourselves and the world—each moment's creativity is a witness to the divine incarnation. We experience God in the vague, emotional, and unconscious feelings that lie at the depths and the edges of our experience—in surprising insights, in dreams, in moments of new awareness, in hunches and intuitions about persons and situations. In each moment of experience, regardless of its complexity, God is present as the gentle persuasion toward growth, beauty, self-awareness, and healing. God is present as the voice that speaks for our deepest and most authentic desires. This gentle, unobtrusive, yet persistent, persuasion of God in each moment of our experience is captured in Paul's words to the Christians in Rome: "Likewise the Spirit helps us in our weakness; for we do not know how to pray as we ought, but that very Spirit intercedes with sighs too deep for words" (Romans 8:26).

God's persuasive love is accordingly the ground of our moment-by-moment experience. Without God's presence within our deepest selves, there would be no direction to our lives, nor could we counter the forces of entropy and disintegration that constantly threaten us. God's faithfulness at the edges of life finds its source in God's intimate presence in each moment of our lives. But God's everpresent aim toward beauty and wholeness is only *one* of the elements conditioning our experience at any moment. God's aim toward beauty and creativity—what traditionally has been called "the will of God"—enters my experience along with countless other impressions, including those of my own past. Accordingly, the impact of God's presence in my life is limited not only by my own freedom but by the wealth of data that confronts me in each moment. Freedom is real. We are always free to turn away from God's ideal for our lives. As the apostle Paul confesses: "I can will what is right, but I cannot do it. For I do not do the good I want, but the evil I do not want is what I do. Now if I do what I do not want, it is no longer I that do it, but sin that dwells within me" (Romans 7:18b–20). Indeed, the lure of the deathful life, what Paul describes as "sin," may virtually blind us to the lively adventure God offers us.

The power of God calls us to growth and transformation. It calls us to let go of the past and be open to the riches of the present moment, but our own need for security or the familiarity of unhealthy patterns of behavior is powerful. We limit what God can do in our lives. Even so, God's steadfast love never gives up on us. God's aim for beauty and growth is specific to each one of us in our own unique set of circumstances. In each new moment, God presents us with an ideal of who we can be in the here and now.

A process-relational vision of God proclaims that although God loves everyone, the particular embodiment of that love varies from moment to moment and from person to person. This is as true for divine parenting as it is for good human parenting. We do not love an infant in the same fashion as we love a recent college graduate. Our response to a child who has awakened from a nightmare is very different from our response to a toddler who is about to run into a busy street. To be contextual and appropriate, God's love, like our own, must be particular and relative. It cannot help but make distinctions. God's aim for a healthy, growing fetus differs from the divine aim for a person who has just received the diagnosis of a life-threatening illness or a person who is comatose. God's aim for someone considering euthanasia as a result of intense pain and isolation differs from God's guidance to one who has just been diagnosed with a highly curable cancer.

Within a process-relational view of God, therefore, it is important to remember that our own willingness to respond to God's call for transformation may either limit or enhance God's own ability to respond to our current needs. A life constantly shaped by fear, rigidity, and denial is a less fertile matrix for God's call forward than a life open to the joy *and* pain of transformation. For some persons, the highest possibility in a given situation may be for them to experience failure, self-judgment, or disillusionment without attempting to repress it. Or, ironically, it may be the release from pain through psychological or chemical anesthesia. But whether God's aim is toward comfort or confrontation, it is always toward that which will eventually promote wholeness, beauty, and integrity within the context of each person's environment and personal history.

Perhaps we need to be reminded that—as Alcoholics Anonymous and other "twelve-step" programs point out—the greatest prelude to creative transformation may be the feeling of total helplessness, of "hitting bottom," which in its starkness turns one toward a power greater than oneself and toward a community of fellow sufferers. God's aim for the realization of beauty may indeed be the source of spiritual and psychological dislocation, whose presence is felt as clearly in *afflicting the comfortable* as in *comforting the afflicted*. Nevertheless, in its many forms, God's faithfulness to us is absolute. God will always give us another chance to live honestly and abundantly. Saul is not left blinded on the road to Damascus. As he confronts the blindness of his old life and the trauma of the new life that awaits him, God provides Saul with a new name, a new vision of reality, and a new community to comfort and challenge him.

God's persuasive presence is similar to the work of an artist. Within the various factors constituting each moment's experience, God seeks intensity, beauty, and adventure by enabling us to break from the past and claim the totality of our experience. Like all artists, however, God respects the integrity of the media. God works to enhance, rather than eliminate, the positive characteristics of each person.

God's love is creative and not destructive in its response to our own freedom and self-creativity. God's love responds to us just as we are. But God invites us to follow the ideal of what we can be. In the experience of a person with AIDS, the divine presence may manifest itself in terms of self-acceptance or as gentle persuasion—a "lure"—toward spiritual growth and openness to friendship rather than a literal physical healing. Such self-forgiveness and openness to the divine may create an environment in which an unexpected healing becomes the aim toward which God next moves. These "Christological moments," discussed in chapter five, are typically described as "miracles." In fact, they are the release of everpresent transformative energies that are heightened when one is fully attuned to the divine aim for oneself and the world. God's presence may be revealed, at one point, in the urge to fight for life. At another time, if one's condition has physically deteriorated, God's presence may be discerned in the call to let go of the fight and prepare for death in trust and grace. Regardless of the situation, God always works sensitively within the totality of our experience, calling each of us forward toward the highest ideal for the present moment, even when its realization may be painful. God is our everpresent source of healing and new life, even when life is ebbing away.

Traditional theologians have seldom identified divine perfection with God's sensitivity and receptivity to the world of change. In fact, the classical tradition has defined change as a defect in God's character. The words "I am the same yesterday, today, and tomorrow" are interpreted to refer solely to the nature of God's unchanging experience rather than to God's unchanging steadfast love. Furthermore, since God's omniscience is usually seen as timeless and eternal rather than as receptive and dynamic, surprise and newness of experience have been judged by the classical tradition to be contrary to the perfection ascribed to divine knowledge. In contrast, I believe that a God whose relationship to the world is only one-directional can hardly be the God of redemptive suffering revealed in the cross of Christ. For God's love of the world to be meaningful, it must be grounded in God's experience of my suffering and joy *from the inside.*

In contrast to the classical tradition, process-relational thought takes divine omniscience seriously. Omniscience means that God truly experiences everything. In contrast to our own finite experience, God's omniscience means that for God everything matters. The sparrow, the grass of the field, the fragile fetus, the starving child, and even the hairs of our heads are known and treasured by God not just as events witnessed from the outside but as feelings experienced from the inside. Our tears and our anguish, our prayers and our doubts, our hopes and our depressions are not lost, but are embraced and treasured in God's own experience. The psalmist's affirmation that God has "searched me and known me" (Psalm 139:1) proclaims that God is far more intimately aware of my life than even my closest friend. I am known by God fully and completely. There is no hiding place from the one "to whom all hearts are open." As the psalmist confesses: "My frame was not hidden from you, when I was being made in secret" (Psalm 139:15). But we need not fear God's knowledge of us, for—unlike our knowledge of one another—God's knowledge is always joined with love.

Put another way, God's relationship to the world is essential to God's own existence. The world truly makes a difference to God. God needs us just as we need God. The fullest expression of love involves receiving as well as giving. In speaking of the significance of the world to God, Whitehead articulates the concept of "the consequent nature of God." Beneath the philosophical language Whitehead employs is the affirmation of the "Galilean vision" of God's love for us.

> By reason of the relativity of all things, there is a reaction of the world on God. The completion of God's nature into the fullness of physical feeling is derived from the objectification of the world in God. He shares with every new creation its actual world; and the concrescent [self-creating] creature is objectified in God as a novel element in God's objectification of that actual world....the consequent nature is the weaving of God's physical feelings upon his primordial concepts.[13]

As radical as it may seem to those enamored by visions of God's independence of the world, process-relational thought maintains that God is incomplete without the world. Creation is not just a divine whim, but is the result of God's own need for companionship and connectedness.

In a world of "perpetual perishing," a world in which the immediacy of the present moment is always fading, God's nature integrates eternity and immediacy. Nothing is ever lost, no tear is ever forgotten, no death is meaningless, for God "saves the world as it passes into the immediacy of His own life."[14] The desire to leave a mark, to make a difference, so essential to our confidence in the face of death, finds its answer not just in the experience of those who succeed us or in our impact on this fragile planet, but in God's own experience of the world which ensures "the unfading importance of our immediate actions, which perish and yet live evermore."[15]

Today our theological reflection must be ecological and holistic in the broadest sense of these words. Interdependence, rather than individualism, must characterize our thinking and acting. Our reflections on God's nature are no exception to the ecological thinking necessary for our time. Authentic companionship is essential for all persons, so that they do not experience deathful living. The process-relational image of God provides the assurance that we are never alone. God is as close to us as our best friend or lover, and our dialogue with God can be just as lively.

The New Testament speaks of the intimacy of Christian community in terms of the "body of Christ" (1 Corinthians 12). In recent times, the intimacy of God and the world has been described in terms of a similar metaphor: the psychosomatic metaphor of the relatedness of mind and body.[16] Just as our minds and bodies exist in a symbiotic relationship of mutual interdependence, God, as the spirit of the world, is intimately influenced by everything in the world. Although the existence of God does not depend absolutely on the particular state of the body, God's experience does reflect the health and disease of the world and each of its creatures. Put another way, the world is "the body of God" and reflects the constant attention of a loving spirit. The term for this view is *panentheism*, meaning that all things dwell in God's experience, but God is not the *sum* of all things, which would characterize pantheism.

For Christians, this means that the imitation of Christ is revealed in our willingness to live by the "Galilean vision" of compassion, connectedness, and reciprocity. To be Christ-like is to be sensitive and open to the lives of other persons. It is to receive as well as to give love. The poetic imagery of William Blake captures the metaphysical, ethical, and personal implications of God's relatedness to the universe.

> Can I see another's woe,
> And not be in sorrow too?
> Can I see another's grief,
> And not seek for kind relief?

Can I see a falling tear,
And not feel my sorrows share?
Can a father see his child
Weep, nor be with sorrow filled?

Can a mother sit and hear
An infant groan, an infant fear:
No, no! Never can it be!
Never, never can it be.

And can he who smiles on all
Hear the wren with sorrows small,
Hear the small bird's grief and care,
Hear the woes that infants bear,

And not sit beside the nest,
Pouring pity on the breast;
And not sit the cradle near,
Wiping tear on infant's fear;

And not sit both night & day;
Wiping all our tears away:
O! Never can it be!
Never can it be!

He doth give his joy to all:
He becomes the infant small;
He becomes a man of woe;
He doth feel the sorrow too.

Think not that thou canst sigh a sigh;
And thy maker is not by:
Think not thou canst wipe a tear,
And thy maker is not near.

O! He gives to us his joy
That our grief he may destroy;
Till our grief is fled and gone
He doth sit by us and moan.[17]

Whitehead's image of the divine invites us to revitalize the Galilean vision of a divinity who saves us through grief and celebration, who "sits by us and moans" and "gives his joy to all." The image of God "as the fellow sufferer who understands" provides the basis for a "metaphysics of love" in which God's power is perfected in suffering (2 Corinthians 12:9–10). A God who creates and receives all reality, including pain and suffering as well as joy and celebration, challenges us to experience both, as God does, simultaneously.

God's power, the power of persuasive love, is grounded in God's sensitivity to the world. God can provide us with a vision of our highest possibilities precisely because God knows us intimately, not only as the source of our experience but also as the one who shares our innermost feelings. As Charles Hartshorne maintains, "God orders the universe, according to panentheism, by taking into his own life all the currents of feeling in existence. He is the most irresistible of influences because he is himself most open to influence."[18] Because God alone knows the depth of our experience from the inside, God alone can provide adequate images of healing for our lives. For example, as God feels the physical and emotional pain of a person with AIDS, God experiences the deep dread, the anticipation of dependence and financial insecurity, and the hope of a cure. In this intimacy of feeling, God is able to enter into the experience of a person diagnosed with a life-threatening illness as *one* of the influences seeking wholeness in the midst of brokenness.

God seeks to respond to our real needs and not some irrelevant or abstract ideal. God's aim toward adventure, beauty, harmony, and intensity of experience is constant and unchanging. However, the form of God's incarnation in the world varies from moment to moment and person to person. When the apostle Paul is afflicted by a "thorn in the flesh," he prays for physical healing. The healing he receives, however, is different and more profound than he sought. As his spirit is healed, he experiences the divine presence as a "grace that is sufficient," which allows him to embrace any hardship that lies ahead. In the incarnation of God in his own experience, Paul discovers that when he is weak, he is truly strong (2 Corinthians 12:7–10).

It is important to note, however, that even in its relativity and interdependence, the relationship of God and the world is such that everything that influences God has already been influenced by God. Our lives contribute to God's experience of the world, and enable God to respond to the world in new and unexpected ways. As limited as our impact may be, we can always, as Mother Teresa of Calcutta proclaims, do "something beautiful for God." Or, as Whitehead puts it:

The kingdom of heaven is with us today. It is the particular providence for particular occasions. What is done in the world is transformed into a reality in heaven, and the reality in heaven passes back into the world. By reason of this reciprocal relation, the love in the world passes into the love in heaven, and floods back again into the world. In this sense, God is the great companion—the fellow sufferer who understands.[19]

Whitehead's description of God as "the fellow sufferer who understands" points to the deepest movements of grace by which all things are created and saved. Not only does God suffer, but God also dies and is reborn in every moment of experience. As the soul of the world, God knows the meaning of perpetual perishing from the inside! There is truly both a cross and a resurrection in the heart of God. The radical continuity of experience, both divine and human, is the matrix within which death and suffering are redeemed and given a meaning in the universe.

As he witnesses the Nazis' execution of a young boy, Elie Weisel is confronted by the reality of evil and the apparent powerlessness of God.

Behind me, I heard the same man asking:
"Where is God now?"
And I heard a voice within me answer him:
"Where is he? Here he is—He is hanging on this gallows."[20]

And we ask, as we see the countless corpses following the disaster in Bangladesh or the starving Somalians in the midst of drought and political anarchy, where is God? If God is not fully present in "the least of these," then God cannot be of any help to us in our moments of anguish and doubt.

The living God continually integrates the past and the present, eternity and adventure, celebration and tragedy. Although nothing is lost in the divine experience, God constantly must let go of past achievements so that the newness of the present might emerge. Eternally creative, God's love must confront anew in each moment the often unexpected and painful realities of the creative process, just as we do. God neither knows nor can fully control the future. Accordingly, the divine aim at beauty and adventure is never static, but always shifting its emphasis in response to the world's needs. "Every act leaves the world with a deeper or fainter impress of God. He then passes into his next relation to the world with enlarged, or diminished, presentation of ideal values."[21] This divine "passing" is the source of both stability and self-transcendence. Indeed, God's fidelity is grounded in God's willingness to die to the past so that the future can be born.

The "history of salvation," manifest in the biblical account of God's continuing covenant with humankind, is a startling revelation to those who hold a vision of a static and all-powerful deity. The emotional, at times confrontational, God of the Old and New Testaments reveals the insight that the God who is "the same yesterday, today, and tomorrow" is also flexible and adventurous in response to the world. God is always doing a new thing. God continually invites us to be part of the adventure. The divine and the human journeys mirror one another: the perfection of the garden gives way to the reality of Abel and Cain and the tower of Babel, and the infinitely ingenious God must shape a vision according to the world that is being experienced by God moment by moment.

Yet, in the face of the world's "imperfection"—the world's ability to say "no" to God—God neither gives up nor condemns humankind to unattainable ideals. Imperfection is part of the very fabric of life. The agony of Christ in the Garden of Gethsemene mirrors the divine grief over the world's lost possibilities and broken dreams. Even when God's chosen one is subjected to death on a cross, God does not abandon humankind. As God's embodiment in our midst, Jesus forgives his persecutors and becomes the vehicle by which God presents the world with an undreamed-of vision of reconciliation and adventure, not only for the persecuted but also for the persecutors as well. Divine perfection is not found in unchanging solitude but in the abundance of possibilities for wholeness and beauty that God offers us in each moment.

In traditional images of God, both eastern and western, God's nature is described in terms of bliss, unity, and changelessness. Such a God is immune not only to change and death in the abstract, but also to the concrete and everyday experiences of change and death. The traditional images of God embody a collective fear of change, pain, and death as well as of intimacy: both the blissful Brahman and the Unmoved Mover find their fulfillment through anesthesia, denial, and emotional withdrawal.

In the process-relational vision of God, on the other hand, God experiences both the death of dreams and the death of persons. God embraces death in God's own infinite sensitivity and openness to the world and to change. The God of process-relational thought is the infinitely related, everchanging, and constantly resourceful God, who is neither immune to nor afraid of death. My pain becomes God's pain, and my joy becomes God's joy, as they are transformed and redeemed within God's experience.

God is "the poet of the world, with tender patience leading it by his vision of truth, beauty, and goodness."[22] While our theme here is adventure at the edges of life, it is not inappropriate to suggest that God's own experience of self-creation and self-transformation is ultimately an adventure in aesthetics. As poet, artist, weaver, and adventurer, God constantly transforms the world within God's own experience. As Whitehead puts it:

> The wisdom of the subjective aim prehends every actuality for what it can be in such a perfected system—its sufferings, its sorrows, its failures, its triumphs, its immediacies of joy—woven by rightness of feeling into the harmony of universal feeling, which is always immediate, always many, always one, always with novel advance, moving onward and never perishing. The results of destructive evil, purely self-regarding, are dismissed into their triviality of merely individual facts; and yet the good they did achieve in individual joy, in individual sorrow, in the introduction of needed contrast, is yet saved by its relation to the completed whole. The image—and it is but an image—the image under which this operative growth of God's nature is best conceived is that of a tender care that nothing be lost....
>
> The consequent nature of God is his judgment on the world. He saves the world as it passes into the immediacy of his own life. It is the judgment of a wisdom which uses what in the temporal world is mere wreckage.[23]

Each moment of the divine experience is the ultimate example of "creative transformation"—the transformation of the world into the aesthetic unity of experience that ceaselessly gives birth to the adventure of the ongoing universe. As artist of the world, God shapes the contrasts of pain and hope, of anguish and consolation, in terms of God's own vision of beauty. With each new moment, though, God self-transforms again and again, shaping and reshaping in response to a new world and God's own emerging aims at beauty and adventure.

God is constantly dying to past hopes in order to be reborn to new hopes. God is never locked in the past. God reaches toward the future through self-transcendence and self-creativity in the present. We can do likewise. In our own participation in the redemption of suffering, we share in God's own experience of the world, giving and receiving, suffering and transforming, dying and giving birth to new life.

To persons at the edges of life, as well as for adventurers along the paths of life, God is truly "the fellow sufferer who understands." In our moments of pain and acceptance, God's omniscience offers us not some timeless and irrelevant vision but a personal and even cosmic empathy. Because God accepts the totality of experience and seeks beauty within the wreckage of our lives, we can take the first steps toward self-acceptance and the discernment of beauty within our own pain and ugliness.

As the artist who holds in contrast hope and hopelessness, pain and wholeness, God invites each drop of experience to embrace the totality of its life—including death and sin—in terms of an adventure toward beauty, harmony, and intensity. God is truly with those who suffer, not as a voyeur or a detached observer, but as one who cries through our tears and rejoices in our laughter, as one whose spirit speaks through our anger and prayers, and as one who invites us to be renewed by the very energy of transformation of God's own experience.

Notes

[1]*The Book of Common Prayer* (New York: Seabury Press, 1979), p. 462.

[2]*Ibid.*, p. 465.

[3]*Ibid.*, p. 483.

[4]Charles Hartshorne and William L. Reese, *Philosophers Speak of God* (Chicago: University of Chicago Press, 1953), p. 73.

[5]Aristotle, *Metaphysics* 1072a. Translated by W.D. Ross and J.A. Smith, *The Works of Aristotle* (Oxford: Clarendon Press, 1917).

[6]*Ibid.*, p. 1074b.

[7]*Ibid.*, p. 99.

[8]Anders Nygren, *Agape and Eros* (Philadelphia: Westminster, 1953), p. 78.

[9]Whitehead, *Process and Reality*, p. 342.

[10]Dietrich Bonhoeffer, *Letters and Papers from Prison* (New York: Macmillan, 1968), p. 188.

[11]John B. Cobb, Jr., *God and the World* (Philadelphia: Westminster Press, 1969), p. 56.

[12]John B. Cobb, Jr., *Christ in a Pluralistic Age* (Philadelphia: Westminster Press, 1975), p. 21.

[13]Whitehead, *Process and Reality*, p. 347.

[14]*Ibid.*, p. 348.

[15]*Ibid.*, p. 351.

[16]Sally McFague, *Models of God* (Philadelphia: Fortress Press, 1987), p. 60.

[17]William Blake, *Songs of Innocence and of Experience* (New York: The Orion Press, 1967), p. 27.

[18]Charles Hartshorne, *Divine Relativity* (New Haven: Yale University Press, 1948), p. xviii.

[19]Whitehead, *Process and Reality*, p. 351.

[20]Elie Weisel, *Night* (New York, Avon Books, 1971), p. 76.

[21]Alfred North Whitehead, *Religion in the Making*, p. 152.

[22]Whitehead, *Process and Reality*, p. 346.

[23]*Ibid.*

4

Death and Our Images
of Health

Mortality and the Quest for Healing

Just a few weeks before I was to have a very important job interview, my son, Matthew, came down with chicken pox. Chicken pox for an eight-year-old is quite normal. However, I had gone through childhood without a case of chicken pox. The prospect of having chicken pox in my mid-thirties filled me with anxiety, especially since the two-week incubation period would exactly coincide with the first day of an important job interview. I sought medical assistance. My physician said there was nothing he could do to prevent the outbreak of chicken pox. I would just have to take my chances. Since I believe in the power of the mind and spirit in health and illness, I spent the next two weeks in extended sessions of prayer and meditation. I also sought the help of alternative healers. In spite of all my efforts, I did not escape chicken pox. However, it did not hit me until the interviews were over and I was on the way home. While chicken pox seems a rather minor inconvenience compared to heart disease or AIDS, I might remind the reader that no illness is

67

unimportant to the persons involved. My experience with chicken pox is not unusual. If we reflect on our lives, most of us will find that we have had numerous experiences in which our state of mind or religious faith made the difference between health and illness.

Each experience of illness drives us to reflect upon our own mortality and the possibilities for the healing of body and spirit. The onset of an illness challenges our naive assumptions about our security and invulnerability. If we are honest, we must admit that being ill forces us to discover our limits and the fragility of our being. Our accustomed sense of connection, bodily integrity, and wholeness is shaken. Like a child kept home from school with the measles, we feel disconnected and envious of those who can play outside, that is, those whose lives seem to go on as usual. Consciously or unconsciously, the symptoms of any illness point beyond themselves to something deeper and more threatening, for every illness provides us with a dress rehearsal for our own dying process. The "mini" death of chicken pox or the flu is the laboratory that compels us to meditate upon our responses to weakness, pain, and the shattering of our comfortable roles in our family or community. Accordingly, the experience of illness is not merely a physical issue. The experience of illness, like that of health, permeates one's whole being, affecting one's body, mind, emotions, and spirit. In our vulnerability, we seek healing not merely for our bodies but for our whole person.

Our search for healing is intimately shaped by our images of God and ourselves. The quest for healing eventually becomes a religious issue.

Today, it is easy to recognize that health and healing are not just individual issues. The setting of chronic illness and death is often institutional. It is obvious that many of us will die in a hospital or nursing home. More salient is the fact that the occurrence of minor and self-limiting illnesses often compels us to seek the assistance of one or more physicians, nurses, chiropractors, spiritual healers, or other holistic health care givers. Both the media and medical profession bombard us with promising new techniques of health and pharmaceutical care. Persons in the Northern Hemisphere have never received so much health care. Our expectations and the claims of health care givers, both orthodox and unorthodox, continue to escalate. In a time when new and unorthodox methods of health care are emerging to match the technology of institutionalized health care, many of us wonder what it truly means to be healthy and how we might take more responsibility for our own health and healing.

In the second and third chapters, personal well-being was identified with wholeness at the edges of life. Personal wholeness is grounded in our openness to the totality of our experience—spiritual, physical, and emotional. While health, like wholeness, varies from person to person, both health and wholeness imply the creative interplay of body, mind, spirit, and relationships, affirmed in the Hebraic concept of *shalom*. Tragically, most of us come to know the meaning of health and wholeness only when we are confronted by the experience of disharmony, disconnectedness, and alienation characterized by illness and sin. Yet our awareness of our brokenness is the invitation to our healing.

Illness in a Technological Age

Simone de Beauvoir's *A Very Easy Death* portrays the painful irony of illness and death in our time. At the age of seventy-seven, Simone de Beauvoir's mother, "Maman," is diagnosed with intestinal cancer during a hospitalization for a fractured femur. Her experience in the hospital is a microcosm revealing the malaise at the heart of technological medicine. Although Madame de Beauvoir receives the finest medical care, she dies in agony, a weak defenseless child, protected and manipulated by modern technology. The euphoric pronouncement of her surgeon, "I have brought her back to life"[1] masks the torture of her final days.

Though the medical diagnosis is terminal cancer, Maman is told it is peritonitis and she rejoices in her imminent recovery. To tell her the truth would deprive her of hope and peace of mind, the doctors counsel. Tragically, Madame de Beauvoir boasts of her remarkable recovery at the very time her life is slipping away from her.

As she awaits her mother's death, Simone de Beauvoir experiences the world as one vast "cancer ward." Simone is tormented not only by the cancer ravaging her mother's body, but also by the "cancer" brought on by her own remorse, grief, and dishonesty. Madame de Beauvoir's illness points to a deeper and more virulent cancer afoot—the cancer that permeates the hospital itself. Although Maman dies "a very easy death," a death under intensive care and with the best treatment available, her death is one of dehumanization and loneliness. She is a victim of the technology created to heal her and the kindness meant to protect her. In her final days, Maman is "reduced by her capitulation to being a body and nothing more, [which] hardly differed from a corpse—a poor defenseless carcass turned and manipulated by professional hands."[2] Although Simone does not want her mother to suffer pain and indignity, she herself capitulates to a medical technology that must prolong life at any cost.

> Dr. N. had been working on Maman: he was going to put a tube into her nose to clean out her stomach. "But what's the good of tormenting her, if she is dying? Let her die in peace," said Poupette in tears....Dr. N. passed by me; I stopped him. White coat, white cap: a young man with an unresponsive face. "Why this tube? Why torture Maman, since there is no hope?" He gave me a withering look. "I am doing what has to be done."[3]

Later, after the "successful" operation, Dr. N. rejoices in his healing powers.

> He was triumphant: she had been half-dead in the morning and yet she had withstood a long and serious operation excellently. Thanks to the very latest methods of anaesthesia, her heart, her lungs, the whole organism had continued to function normally. There was no sort of doubt that he entirely washed his hands of the consequences of that feat.[4]

Dr. N. had brought Maman back to life. But beneath the triumph of modern medicine, Simone asks herself: "For what?"[5]

A Very Easy Death is a microcosm of our own ambivalence as we reflect upon health and illness in our time. In spite of the marvels of modern technology, the contemporary health care movement is diseased. The human element, the element of the spirit and values, has been exorcised from the hospital and the contemporary medical model. The death of Madame de Beauvoir reveals not only the limits of technology but also the dark side of a medical model oriented solely toward bodily illness and the avoidance of death at any cost.

In this chapter I will reflect on the interplay of death, health, and healing, first by discussing the shortcomings of the modern biomedical model of health care. Then, constructively, I will present a vision of holistic or psychosomatic health—first from the perspective of medicine, incorporating the thought of three physicians, Eric Cassell, O. Carl Simonton, and Bernie Siegel, and then from the perspective of theology, building on the insights of Paul Tillich. Following these preliminary reflections, I will outline a process-relational model of health that will provide a foundation not only for the transformation of contemporary health care but also for the inclusion of the entirely new holistic visions of health, currently emerging at the fringes of institutional medicine. Chapter five will consider the possibility of spiritual or faith healing within this same process-relational perspective.

The issue of health, medicine, and healing is an issue of faith as well as of science. The biblical understanding of life, most evident in the healing ministry of Jesus, affirms that our response to God's presence is reflected in our bodies as well as in our spirits. If God is present in all things, then physical as well as spiritual responses to illness ultimately reveal the interplay of God's activity and the human response.

Voices of Discontent:
The Need for a New Medical Model

How we see health and healing is, in part, shaped by the predominant mythology or worldview by which our culture lives. The "mythology" around illness and death in our culture serves as an unconscious lens through which we experience and understand our world. Accordingly, our implicit understanding of reality defines not only what we see but also what we deem possible.

The vision of health by which we live does not emerge from a vacuum but involves the integration of personal experience, medical practice, and underlying cultural and religious assumptions. Fortunately for us, our culture's vision of health, like its vision of death, is in flux. Images of health and medical care abound, and this diversity challenges us to synthesize the rich and often seemingly incoherent range of perspectives. We need to explore new images of death, health, and medicine on a personal as well as institutional level.

In its current practice, modern medicine reflects both the divine and the demonic aspects of the human technological adventure. Health and illness have always had religious dimensions. Throughout the ages, persons have sought out priests, shamans, witches, midwives, and physicians to be their advocates against the forces of disharmony and destruction. The skill and expertise of the physician or other healer makes the difference not only between life and death but also between health and disability. The religious aura surrounding contemporary medicine is revealed by the comments of a woman suffering from rheumatic heart disease. When her physician, Eric Cassell, asked her, "What is a doctor's job?" she replied:

> To keep me alive—and more....Because especially now, I don't believe in God anymore really and truly. So the doctor's job is one that never existed before—far beyond any of the others. There were some gods that took care of everything, there was Jesus....There was once another world, but since I don't believe in it anymore, for me the doctor is now God....All the things that were asked of gods, essentially what were they? Even if the Aztecs let the blood out, it was to give more life. Now there is only the doctor to protect me from the things around us.[6]

As the technological heir of the shaman, medicine man, and high priest, the contemporary physician is a bearer of power in the human struggle against the forces of entropy, death, and darkness. Indeed, like the shaman of old, the physician is called to cure the sick and accompany the dying to the "other world." In this context, the godlike role of the physician and the numinous quality of the medical art and its central shrine, the modern hospital, is understandable. In a world in which God appears absent and death has become a "lost season," William F. May suggests that only evil and the forces of destruction have "sufficient energy, vitality, and allure to make headlines and command attentiveness."[7] Accordingly, the "modern doctor's authority derives chiefly from a grim negativity, that is, from the fear of suffering and death, and from the retaliatory powers that modern biomedical research puts at his or her disposal."[8] To a vulnerable, defenseless, and isolated patient, who no longer believes in the presence or power of God, the tools and techniques of the physician promise life, hope, and comfort.

Today's predominant image of health and medicine—hereafter referred to as the biomedical model—has given great hope and comfort to humankind. It has provided an armory of valuable techniques and technologies for the curing of the human body. From the perspective of the biomedical model, health is ultimately a matter of physical existence and the proper functioning of the body and its organs. This "somatic" or body orientation is the basis of its power in the quest for healing and transformation. Tragically, however, this same orientation also prevents the biomedical model from addressing the spiritual and emotional needs of the sick and dying.

According to the biomedical model, illness, like health, pertains primarily to physical existence. Illness is defined in terms of the breakdown of normal bodily functions, which must be addressed somatically through chemicals, radiation, or surgery. Although physicians recognize the growing interest in psychosomatic or holistic medicine and the unexpected beneficial effects of placebos on patient recovery, most physicians still see issues of belief systems, emotional health, family patterns, work, and recreational lifestyle as unimportant to health care and the medical practice. When issues of the emotions and belief systems arise, they are typically dismissed as secondary phenomena and transferred to another discipline (for example, psychotherapy, social work, or pastoral care). From the perspective of the biomedical model, human well-being is synonymous with proper physical functioning and personal comfort. The person who seeks the services of the contemporary physician is often bombarded with physical solutions to spiritual and emotional issues. A proper and appropriate combination of diet, vitamins, exercise, plastic surgery, and chemical therapy will ensure, the consumer is told, a long, healthy, and happy life. If one happens to neglect the body, the physician, like a good mechanic, will "repair" the dysfunctional parts.

As a mirror of the biomedical vision of health, medical education focuses almost exclusively on scientific technique, pathological diagnosis, and crisis medicine. Issues in preventive medicine, human relations, death and dying, and ethical decision making are of peripheral concern. Despite the fact that most illnesses are routine and self-limiting in nature, the young physician and the public in general are educated to believe that good medical care pertains solely to the well-being of the body and is almost completely a result of the expertise of the physician, the hospital, and the available technology. This "belief system" promotes passivity and victimization among persons, who appropriately are called "patients." The mythology of modern health is most evident in the hospital, the shrine of somatic technology, the place where the war on disease is undertaken. Here, in the midst of CAT scans and MRIs, inoculations and serums, radiation and chemotherapy, the fearful and broken seek healing.

In response to those who see my critique of modern health care as harsh and negative, I must confess that my interest in a new medical model has grown out of my friendship with physicians, my teaching of medical and nursing students, and my appreciation of the commitment to excellence of the physicians who have served my family. My desire is for health care, in all its forms, truly to become an instrument of healing.

Despite the marvels of modern medical technology, I believe that there is growing awareness of the dark and sinister side of the contemporary vision of health. At the institutional level there is increased patient dissatisfaction with rising health care costs, impersonal treatment, and the negative side effects of surgery and chemical therapy. The dark side of the biomedical model is most evident at the edges of life. In the face of death, the shortcoming of its somatic orientation and the neglect of emotional, valuational, and spiritual issues add to the loneliness of the dying. Although persons with life-threatening illnesses live much longer today than in previous times, mere "quantity" of time may eventuate in severely limited "quality" of life. This reality is reflected in the decreased fear of death itself and increased fear of the process of dying! When curing becomes an impossibility, the somatic physician feels helpless as she faces a terminally ill patient. Pain relief and "intensive care" is often all the hospital can offer.

The roots of the current biomedical crisis lie in its philosophical foundations. In a highly influential article, Professor George Engel maintains that the crisis in modern medicine originated from the "adherence to a model of disease no longer adequate for the scientific task and social responsibilities of either medicine or psychiatry."[9] The biomedical model, according to Engel, "embraces both reductionism, the philosophic view that complex phenomena are ultimately derived from a single primary principle, and mind-body dualism, the doctrine that separates the mental from the somatic."[10]

Engel and many other historians of medicine trace the modern vision of health to the influence of the seventeenth century philosopher, René Descartes. Descartes divided reality into two distinct and unrelated substances, the mind and the body. Whereas the mind is spiritual and creative, the body is material and mechanistic. While the spirit, or mind, may encounter God, the body relates to its Creator only indirectly. Descartes' division of reality and human existence into mental and physical spheres played an essential role in the rise of modern medicine. As purely material and mechanical, the body could be manipulated, dissected, and studied organ by organ. Yet the body was devoid of feelings, subjectivity, and religious relevance.

In the division of reality influenced by Descartes, the church was given the care of the mind and spirit, while the scientist and physician received custody of the body. Neither was to intrude on the other's territory. Like the deists he inspired, Descartes saw the physical world, and the human body, as akin to a clock, crafted by a distant and unrelated creator. A healthy body is like a well-made clock, while a sick body is analogous to a poorly made or badly treated clock.

As purely mechanical and material, the body could be treated piecemeal, one organ at a time, without regard to emotions, thoughts, or even other bodily organs. The body was a machine. Disease represented a breakdown in the machine. The doctor's task was primarily to repair what had been broken. The spirit, like the driver of a car being serviced at the shop, lay beyond the expertise and the interest of the medical "mechanic."

However, the development of the biomedical model does not end with the influence of Descartes. The clarity and analytic precision, central to Descartes' philosophy, eventually led to the total elimination of the soul and God from issues of science, health, and human experience. After all, who has seen God or measured the soul? Spirituality, when it was addressed at all, was confined to narrowly defined issues of faith, ethics, and the afterlife. There was no longer any place for prayer or divine activity in the physical world. By the nineteenth century, even the existence of God and the mind became dubious to many educated persons. The mind, once exalted as humankind's participation in the divine, was now understood merely as a reflection of one's physiological state. What we describe as spiritual and emotional issues are ultimately somatic issues, affected by neurological alterations and cured by chemical therapy or behavior modification.

Although the biomedical model traces its origins to the quest for clarity and simplicity, its philosophical simplicity is bought at the price of neglecting humanity's deepest emotional, moral, and spiritual intuitions. It is time to rethink the biomedical model and the philosophical worldview it presupposes, not merely because it is outdated and inadequate for the age of relativity theory and quantum physics but, more importantly, because its rigid employment may actually harm those it most faithfully seeks to help.

The philosopher Gottfried Leibniz once said that "philosophers err more in what they deny than in what they affirm." This is certainly true of the principles underlying the biomedical model. There is no need to jettison the lifesaving technological advances of our time. Rather, the technological vision of modern medicine requires a broader and more holistic, indeed a more empirical, perspective that combines analysis with synthesis, rationality with intuition, treatment with prevention, curing with compassion, and humanism with specialization. A more inclusive perspective would affirm the role of emotions and spirituality in health care and would expand the "team" of healers to include, more intentionally, pastors and psychologists, spiritual guides and healing touch practitioners, herbalists and spiritual healers, as well as physicians and nurses and the patients themselves. In so doing, medicine and the cultural image of health would overcome its major weaknesses: its fragmentation and undue specialization, its focus on one-cause/one-disease thinking, its neglect of the role of the patient in health and illness, and its preoccupation with disease rather than health.

A new vision of health and medicine is ultimately an issue of faith and belief systems, rather than technical expertise. As I have pointed out, the biomedical model and its philosophical foundation ultimately reflect a particular vision of reality and a specific object of faith. Modern medicine is often criticized for its disease orientation. Indeed, the imperative to maintain extraordinary treatment in order to gain time for the patient is symptomatic of a deeper metaphysical issue: the belief that the world is at best indifferent, if not hostile, to human existence, and that the universe provides no resources for healing beyond our human efforts. This is the most basic question of human life as well as health care. Are we alone in the universe? Are death and suffering the ultimate evils humanity faces? Are the forces of evil and disintegration stronger than the forces of creativity and healing? Is there a power within reality that seeks healing and wholeness at the edges of life?

If God and spirituality are irrelevant to health care, then modern medicine can define itself only in negative terms as a war against death and illness. From such an adversarial position, death and illness are meaningless, yet overwhelming.They cannot be accepted or learned from, but must be fought to the very end, even if the patient's well-being is sacrificed in the process. As one physician confesses,

> The medical imperative...is to apply one temporary relief after another, stretching the life of a patient with cancer of the bowel to ten months, who would have died within weeks if any one massive remedy had not been used. To the question, "When should the physician stop treating the patient?," there can be but one answer: "He must carry on until the issue is taken out of his hands."[11]

But the issue is always finally taken out of our hands. In the face of inevitable death, the imperative to preserve life leaves in its wake Simone de Beauvoir's question, "For what?" If meaningless death is the greatest enemy, then our attempts at healing are always fraught with anxiety and the fear of failure.

Ultimately I believe that we live by our affirmations rather than our negations. A medicine ruled by negativity, illness, and mistrust of the universe and the healing resources inherent in human life is unable to address our deepest needs both as healthy persons and as persons with life-threatening illnesses. When death is perceived as the ultimate enemy, its occurrence is always a defeat and a challenge to the very existence of medicine itself.

Evil, pain, and suffering do abound. We cannot, like the Christian Scientists, deny their existence. However, we must also affirm that the dark side does not constitute the whole picture. An affirmative and inclusive model of medicine responds dynamically to pain and suffering. But its fight is grounded in an overall trust in the healing resources of nature, the patient, and the divine reality itself. As my wife's chiropractor continually stresses, "the power that made the body heals the body." A constructive and affirmative vision of health and medicine focuses first on prevention and empowerment and then on intervention. A process-relational worldview enables us to become creative partners in the process of health, prevention, and recovery. Ownership of health is an enterprise for all of us, not just for the "professionals." Health and illness are recognized as issues relating not only to us as individuals but also to the wider institutional and community environment. From a wider perspective, the prospect of death brings forth feelings of empathy and challenge as well as feelings of fear and anger. Even at the edges of life, we are encouraged to discover reasons to live and thus not only to defy the odds but gain the inspiration to die with grace and dignity.

The challenge for a more inclusive model of medicine, health, and wellness comes to us not only from the spiritual and philosophical realms but also from biology and the new physics. In an age of relativity theory, much of modern medicine still operates according to principles set forth by Newton and Descartes. In the context of new images of the universe and the human body, a Christian process-relational vision of reality, ecological and holistic as it is, provides the most adequate and open-ended foundation for the transformation of health and healing in our time. Inspired by a vision of God, the world, and human existence as dynamic and relational in nature, this vision of reality is able to synthesize and integrate not only the body and mind, but the many forms of health care emerging in our time.

Voices of Transformation: Cassell, Siegel, and Simonton

Today a shift is beginning to occur within the medical community. Physicians are beginning to listen to their patients. Medical students are beginning to ask questions about values, ethics, and spirituality. The pride of the "technician" and the "fighter" is giving way to a willingness to accept alternative images of health and health care. Some physicians and health care givers are discovering that they must transcend the artificially imposed limits of their professions in order to fulfill their vocation as healers. These adventurers within the medical profession are exploring the frontiers of meditation, acupuncture, hypnosis, and spiritual healing in the treatment of their patients.

In this section we will explore the expanding horizons of health care as envisaged by some medical practitioners themselves. Any constructive vision of health and health care, especially at the edges of life, must take into account the reflections of those who are most committed to the integration of technical medicine with the exploration of the healing powers residing in each person. Within the medical community, Eric Cassell, O. Carl Simonton, and Bernie Siegel exemplify this search for personal and medical transformation.

Eric Cassell, an internist and professor at the Columbia University Medical School, critiques the biomedical model from within the tradition itself. Cassell's work is dominated by the belief that physicians are called to heal persons as well as to cure diseases. According to Cassell, the dominant belief of the medical subculture is disease.[12] The negative focus of medicine, revealed in its disease-orientation, along with the mind-body dualism so influential in the medical worldview, has led to the eclipse of the role of physician as healer. While curing deals primarily with organs, healing addresses the whole person. Cassell holds that a disease is something an organ has, while illness is something a person has. Yet few physicians and laypersons recognize this subtle difference. Disease can be objectively enumerated in terms of organs, blood pressure, and blood counts. But physical symptoms and diseased organs cannot fully account for the dislocation, vulnerability, and anxiety felt subjectively by the sick. Illness relates to the totality of my experience and not just to my body. Accordingly, medicine is an inherently moral and relational profession, which must address emotional and personal as well as physical needs. The physician must always resist the temptation of solving moral issues by technological means.[13] Since doctors do not treat diseases but persons who have diseases, the physician's focus must include healing as well as curing, personal empowerment as well as technical expertise. As a healer, the physician seeks to enable her patients to regain the sense of confidence and control in their lives.

While the nontechnical side of medicine is important in every healing encounter, it is especially significant in the care of the dying. A disease-oriented medicine eventually debilitates both the physician and the patient: the physician is a failure, the patient is abandoned. According to Cassell, "the physician who sees his only role as the curer of disease or the battler against death is often helpless; the physician who knows that his task is to help the sick to the limit of his ability is almost always able to offer something."[14] At the edges of life, when the fighter and technician have given up, the physician as healer and adventurer is able "to protect the sick from helplessness, fear, and loneliness, agonies that are worse than death."[15] In contrast to customary practice, Cassell believes that the physician may be called upon to create an environment in which she teaches the patient how to die. "When the patient has control over the process of dying, alleviation of pain and distress is possible and dying well becomes a meaningful and positive reality."[16] When the time for fighting has ended, the physician is called upon not only to stop the application of technology but also "to actively help the dying patient develop the will to die."[17] According to Cassell, "it is possible to suggest to the patient that the time has come to leave, but at the same time it is necessary to reassure the patient that it is all right to leave and that it is not going to hurt."[18]

In order to accompany her patient on the journey toward death, the physician must be acutely aware of her own mortality as well as the limits and possibilities of medical care. Such a physician is aware of the forgotten truth that "one of the most important tools of medicine is the physician himself. Medicine is concerned with the care of persons by persons, as simple as that."[19] When the physician allows herself to be a channel of healing, she is able to elicit the healing resources within her patient, even when death is the most likely outcome. Although his work is not explicitly religious in tone, Cassell's image of medical care is a testimony to the fact that technological expertise need not exclude humanitarian care and that objectivity can be integrated with a concern for values both in the practice of medicine and in the person of the physician.

The work of O. Carl Simonton, a radiation oncologist, and Bernie Siegel, a surgeon, has opened new pathways for holistic health and patient empowerment. Like Kübler-Ross, Simonton and Siegel have attempted to address the concerns of laypersons as well as physicians, nurses, and academics. Although their patient-by-patient approach to medical documentation has been criticized by members of the medical establishment, their work has enabled many persons facing chronic and terminal illness to experience hope, the recovery of health, and lively death. Simonton and Siegel have explored the relationship between cancer, hope, and empowerment.

Cancer, as Robert Cantor has suggested, is the most feared disease of our time. Although cardiovascular disease accounts for nearly 50 percent of all deaths in the United States, compared to less than 17 percent for cancer, we are, as a society and as individuals, terrified by cancer. According to some surveys, the prospect of cancer is more terrifying than either violent crime or nuclear war.[20] Chaotic and uncontrollable, cancer symbolizes the random and irrational shadow side of human existence. Even the institutional "fight" against this disease provides little comfort. Many patients are afraid of the disfigurement, loss of social standing, and chronic pain that accompanies cancer. In many cases the treatment is more traumatic than the illness itself.[21] Before the irrational and shadowy aggression of cancer, we feel helpless and victimized. Even our descriptions of cancer go beyond the medical to the existential and the metaphorical. The following examples from leading medical authorities reveal the profound social mythology surrounding cancer.

> For some unknown reason, one cell changes and begins to reproduce in a wild and disorderly way. They become hungrier, steal nourishment from their normal neighbors and crowd them out.

> Cancer is one of the most intractable, variable and incomprehensible forms of cellular derangement. A cancer is a crab as its name indicates. It claws at us, it hides in the sands of our flesh; like a crab, it ignores straight walking, progresses sideways in its refusal to behave in an honest, purposeful manner, and in its need to invade neighboring tissues and to shoot some of its cells far away from its point of origin.[22]

Negative beliefs about cancer as a "dark and many-headed deadly monster" hold our culture in their grip far worse than the disease itself. Despite advances of medicine in the treatment of cancer, for many persons the disease still symbolizes meaningless death, personal powerlessness, and, ultimately, the demonic. The appeal of Simonton and Siegel is due greatly to their willingness to confront the prevalent myths of cancer and thereby to enable persons to become actors and creators rather than victims of death.

At the heart of O. Carl Simonton's approach is the recognition that "we all participate in our health through our beliefs, our feelings, and our attitudes toward life, as well as in more direct ways, such as exercise and diet."[23] In contrast to images of cancer that encourage victimization and impotence, Simonton maintains:

> It is our central premise that an illness is not purely a physical problem but a problem of the whole person, that it includes not only body but mind....emotional and mental states play a significant role in the susceptibility to disease, including cancer, and the recovery from all disease.[24]

Simonton's holistic perspective emphasizes the importance of personal responsibility for both health and illness. This is especially evident in his studies of the origins of cancer. According to Simonton, the origins of cancer in a particular person cannot fully be explained in terms of the traditional "one cause" approach (that is, the identification of cancer solely with radiation, carcinogens, genetics, or diet). An exhaustive explanation of the incidence of cancer must also deal with the "suppression of the body's natural defense against disease," especially since "when exposed to cancer-producing substances, most people still remain healthy."[25]

Simonton suggests that the prevention of and recovery from cancer involve recognizing the importance of the immune system in the origins of the disease. Normally, the body's own immune system recognizes and destroys cancer cells. For cancer to occur, Simonton believes, the effectiveness of the immune system must be inhibited. Simonton believes that this inhibition of the immune system is primarily psychological and emotional: there is a link between stress and illness. Excessive and unrelieved stress, due to hopelessness, fear, or anxiety, suppresses the immune system and creates imbalances in the hormonal systems. This can occur at the most subtle and unconscious levels! The suppression of the immune system not only increases susceptibility to illness but also the production of abnormal cells.[26] Based on their understanding of the role of the immune system in sickness and health, Simonton and others have suggested that the occurrence of cancer is related to our interpretation of ourselves and the world.

Studies by Carl Simonton and others provide growing evidence of certain psychohistorical precursors to the diagnosis of cancer. In the origins of cancer, philosophical and psychological factors may be as significant as somatic and environmental factors. According to Simonton, the precursors to cancer include:

1. Negative experiences in childhood, which result in the conscious or unconscious decision to become a certain kind of person, that is, to have a particular orientation toward oneself and the world.
2. The individual, in later life, is shaken by a cluster of stressful experiences such as divorce, death, or loss of employment.
3. The stresses create a problem the individual cannot respond to, within the limits of his or her current interpretation of self and reality.
4. The individual feels trapped and unable to change.
5. The individual avoids the problem, becoming static, rigid, and unchanging.[27]

The human organism, however, is predisposed toward change, fluidity, and growth. Despite the person's wishes, something changes, something grows—in this case, cancer cells. The constellation of responses and interpretations of reality, including the repression of emotions, feelings of victimization, lack of trust in oneself and the world, and a focus on the past rather than the future, paves the way for the breakdown of the immune system.

For Simonton, the individual whose hopelessness has played a role in her or his susceptibility to cancer or other life-threatening illnesses may also become an agent in the prevention and remission of cancer. Recovery from cancer requires a change in one's interpretation of oneself, the world, and the cancer. In contrast to the demonic descriptions of cancer as invasive, all-powerful, and irrational, Simonton counsels a reinterpretation of the nature of cancer. Cancer cells are, in fact, weak and confused, unable to perform their intended function. In contrast to the aimless cancer cells, the fully functioning immune system is able to recognize and destroy these random cells.[28]

Recovery also requires challenging the mythology of cancer and its negative belief system. Once again, we must hear the "bad news" before we can embrace the "good news." The prevalent mythology of cancer holds that (1) cancer is synonymous with death, (2) cancer is something that strikes from without and there is no hope in controlling it, and (3) treatment always is drastic and has undesirable side effects.[29] Healing requires a change of attitude and behavior, a transformation of consciousness, in which hope and empowerment replace helplessness and victimization.

In addition to medical treatment, Simonton's patients participate in psychotherapy and learn meditation techniques. The process of personal transformation involves:

1. a new perspective on their problems;
2. a decision to alter behavior and become a different kind of person;
3. experiencing new physical and psychological well-being, as physical processes change in response to transformed perceptions and emotions;
4. experiencing oneself as "weller than well" as a result of one's renewed commitment to growth and personal power.

Physical recovery results from treating the body and the mind as an integral whole. Indeed, Simonton affirms that a "positive attitude toward treatment was a better predictor of response to treatment than was the severity of disease."[30]

The psychosomatic unity of disease and health is revealed in Simonton's use of meditation and visualization in the treatment of what traditionally has been reserved to surgery, radiation, and chemotherapy alone. Visualization and meditation, as studies of biofeedback have demonstrated, reduce stress and empower the immune system in its response to disease. As part of medical protocol, Simonton encourages patients to visualize the cancer, the treatment destroying it, and the body's defenses helping the patient recover. One patient, for example, saw the radiation therapy as

> consisting of tiny bullets of energy that would hit all the cells, both normal and cancerous, in their path. Because the cancer cells were weaker and more confused than normal cells, they would not be able to repair the damage...and so the normal cells would remain healthy while the cancer cells would die.[31]

Another patient whose terminal cancer progressively disappeared following his participation in Simonton's program was asked "to form a mental picture of the white blood cells coming in, swimming over the cancer cells, picking up and carrying off the dead and dying ones, flushing them out of his body through the liver and kidneys."[32] In the response to cancer, the aggressive urge toward health, motivated by a changed lifestyle and

sense of personal self-affirmation and assertiveness, brings healing where only death seemed likely.

The psychosomatic vision of health and illness, advocated
by Simonton, encourages a creative synthesis of technical medicine with concern for emotions and personal values. In so doing, a new approach to treatment emerges, based on the recognition that: (1) illness and health have emotional and psychological components, and (2) each person is an agent in her or
his own well-being. Although Simonton's work is nonsectarian
in nature, it is obvious that the Christian affirmation of a power
in the universe that wills wholeness and healing in our lives can
be a creative factor in our response to life-threatening illness.

Bernie Siegel, a surgeon and professor of medicine at Yale
Medical School, sees his work in the treatment of persons with
cancer as an elaboration of the work of O. Carl Simonton. However, for Siegel, the primary factor in health and illness is love.
According to Siegel, "all disease is ultimately related to a lack
of love, or love that is only conditional....all healing is related to
the ability to give and accept unconditional love."[33] Love and its
absence have physiological consequences: in the "mind-body
connection," feelings are chemical and can cure or kill.[34] "The
emotions are everywhere in the body, not just in the brain....they
are expressed in the body and are part of the body."[35] Further,
Siegel holds that "body and mind are different expressions of
the same information—the information carried by the chemical
transmitters known as peptides."[36] The mind-body connection,
integrated through the relationship of the nervous and endocrine
systems, is rooted in the basic constitution of the human being.

In contrast to the biomedical tradition, whose focus on disease is grounded in fear and negativity, Siegel believes that the
primary focus of medicine should be to nurture and empower
the drive toward healing within each person. The human quest
for love and healing does not exist in a cosmic vacuum. Rather,
the force behind creation is a loving, intelligent energy, which
enables us to find peace and resolve conflict. Siegel identifies
spirituality with self-acceptance and the recognition of the energy of healing and creativity that permeates oneself—body,
mind, and emotions—as well as the universe. In opening to this
healing energy, the proper attitude toward cancer and other life-
threatening diseases is, ironically, love and acceptance.

Whereas Simonton's early work often involved counseling
his patients to envisage battles between aggressive white cells

and disorganized cancer cells, Siegel believes that even the desire to kill one's cancer cells may be a form of self-hatred, or a direct attack on one's own self. Healing comes from loving one's whole self, even the cancer and the AIDS. In responding to his cancer, one patient "visualized the appropriate immune cells gently carrying the cancer cells away and instead of killing them, flushing them out of his body."[37]

In his work, Siegel suggests that both human health and the practice of medicine exist in a wider "cosmic" context and that illness and wholeness reflect our response to the omnipresent healing energies always at our disposal. Siegel's concept of healing synthesizes religion and medicine, soft touch and high technology, tradition and novelty. Although Siegel does not specifically identify himself with the Jewish or Christian traditions, his recognition that the healing power of love is both personal and cosmic affirms the Christian insight that the world is a reflection of God's active and abiding love.

The exploration of the emotional and spiritual dimensions of life, articulated by Cassell, Simonton, and Siegel, points toward the importance of the transcendent dimension in medicine and helps us discern the philosophical and religious foundations for the new visions of health and human wholeness.

Christianity as the Meaning of Health: Paul Tillich

Christian faith has always been concerned with the healing of the body and spirit. The psychosomatic unity of life and its relationship to health and illness is evident in the counsels of the Letter of James to the early church:

> Are any among you sick? They should call for the elders of the church and have them pray over them, anointing them with oil in the name of the Lord. The prayer of faith will save the sick, and the Lord will raise them up; and anyone who has committed sins will be forgiven. Therefore confess your sins to one another, and pray for one another, so that you may be healed.
>
> James 5:14–16a

Despite the holistic spirituality of the early church and its founder, the concern for physical healing was soon subordinated to the concern for the afterlife. Over several centuries, the focus of attention moved from the care of the whole person, body and spirit, to the care and preparation of the soul in light of its eternal destiny. The "Galilean vision" of care for the totality of life was eclipsed, except at the edges of institutional Christianity. Healings still occurred. But there was little room for them in either the theology or the practice of the church.

Since the time of Descartes, Christianity has generally abdicated its role in the healing of bodies. In the last few centuries, pastoral care has focused primarily on more narrowly defined spiritual issues such as the preparation for the afterlife, the forgiveness of sins, and personal growth. Although some contemplative prayer disciplines have emphasized spiritual empowerment and the care for others, seldom have they addressed physical needs. Despite their concern for the practical applications of faith, nineteenth- and twentieth-century religious activists have continued this dualistic trend in their emphasis on one-dimensional political and economic answers for human liberation issues. Just as eighteenth-century pietism erred in its overemphasis on the inner life, the social gospel and its contemporary heirs have often erred in their continuing overemphasis on the objective and external implications of faith.

With the exception of groups such as Sojourners and the Church of the Savior in Washington, D.C., churches and Christian organizations have continued to compartmentalize the spheres of spirituality, politics, and physical well-being. Mainstream Christianity has left the realm of physical healing to gnostic movements such as Christian Science or to Pentecostal faith healers who often see healing as an arbitrary act of God, programmed to appear on stage. While pioneers such as Granger Westberg of the Wholistic Health Centers and Cicely Saunders of St. Christopher's Hospice have explored the frontiers of spirituality and health, mainline Christianity has lagged behind psychotherapy and, it seems, even medicine in its exploration of the psychosomatic unity of health and illness. Pastors and lay caregivers alike have received little direction, apart from communication skills and psychological training, in their attempts to minister to the needs of the sick and dying. In spite of the biblical heritage of prayer and spiritual healing, pastors and Christian friends have struggled with the theological and practical implications of prayer and divine activity at the edges of life. When we have prayed with the sick, we have often done so with feelings of uncertainty, embarrassment, and futility. But the fact of prayer itself, in all its ambiguities, reveals our quest to experience the energies of a higher power within our lives. Today the church cries out for an integrative Christian vision to serve as a basis for a practical spirituality of health and healing.

Among mainline Christians, the growing interest in holistic health owes much to the German-American theologian Paul Tillich's attempts to integrate psychology, health, and spirituality in the Christian understanding of human existence. Tillich's work provides the broad outlines of the practical theology of health and healing presented in this and the next chapter.

At the heart of Tillich's understanding of health and healing is the belief that salvation, wholeness, and integration are basically "cosmic" events.[38] In the human body, the soul, the nation, or the cosmos, salvation is "basically and essentially healing, the reestablishment of a whole that was broken, disrupted, and disintegrated."[39] Accordingly, issues of salvation cannot be restricted to the soul alone but must include the whole person and her or his social and cosmic environment.

Tillich's notion of salvation as multidimensional is rooted in his understanding of human existence. Human existence is a "multidimensional unity," which includes all the dimensions of life. According to Tillich, the doctrine of multidimensional unity "stands against the dualistic theory which sees man as composed of soul and body; or body and mind; or body, soul, and spirit."[40] All the dimensions of life penetrate one another and, thus, affect one another. As an intellectual forerunner of the current movements in holistic health, Tillich maintains that health and disease, insofar as they relate to the whole person, are psychosomatic. Disease or health, in any dimension of life, affects all the others. Health, then, cannot be understood as merely physical or merely individual in nature. There are no sharp lines between the health of body and spirit or the health of persons and nations. Threats to the ecosphere, for example, unconsciously influence the physical and psychic health of each individual human.

From the perspective of the multidimensional unity of life, authentic healing includes every dimension of life. Tillich, like Cassell, suggests that it is possible to cure the disease yet leave the patient broken. "Unhealthy health" occurs when "healing under one dimension is successful but does not take into account the other dimensions in which health is lacking or even imperiled by a particular healing."[41] Long before the rise of the holistic health movement, Tillich pointed out that "successful surgery may produce psychological trauma, effective drugs may calm down an uneasy conscience and preserve a moral deficiency...the converted Christian may suffer under repressions which produce fanaticism and explode in lawless forms."[42] Even "the well trained, athletic body may contain a neurotic personality,"[43] or, as we have found out in recent years, be imprisoned due to abuse of drugs, alcohol, or steroids.

Tillich believes that the multidimensional nature of life requires the envisagement of a multidimensional health care system in which religious and medical healing find a common ground.

> If salvation is understood in the sense of healing, there is no conflict between the religious and the medical, but the most intimate relation. Only a theology which has forgotten this relation, and sees salvation as the elevation of the individual to a heavenly place, can come into conflict with medicine. And only a medicine which denies the non-biological dimensions in life their significance for the biological dimension (including its physical and chemical conditions) can come into conflict with theology.[44]

Yet the multidimensional unity of health does not imply perfection or immortality. Health and illness are never absolute or static in nature. They are processes that always exist on a dynamic continuum, insofar as they reflect the ambiguity of creation and destruction that characteristizes all of life. Tillich reminds those who would trust in the technical or unorthodox wonders of our time that "healing is fragmentary in all its forms. Manifestations of disease struggle continuously with manifestations of health....not even the healing power of the Spirit can change this situation."[45] Accordingly, in a world characterized at every level by sin and brokenness, the physician and religious healer alike are challenged to accept the presence of death even amid their "successes," and to discover ways in which they can nurture the overall well-being of persons even at the jagged edges of their lives. Although death and disease are inevitable realities, they need not be failures for the healer who addresses the whole person.

Tillich's vision of the multidimensional unity of life provides a rudimentary foundation for Christian exploration into the mysterious interplay of body and spirit, health and illness. A process-relational vision builds on Tillich's insights in the articulation of a more inclusive map of the realms of health, disease, and healing. In so doing, process thought provides an insightful framework for the emerging insights of holistic health and medicine as well as for understanding the presence of God in the healing of persons.

The Process-Relational View of Health

Process thought represents a sustained critique of mechanistic, dualistic, and atomistic thinking. It is clear to me that if the necessary transformation of the current medical model of health is to take place, it must be based on a unitive process-relational system of beliefs. Such a system of beliefs allows us to integrate without hesitation the newest discoveries on the frontiers of medical science, spirituality, and psychology. As part of the rich fabric of long-standing theological reflection and religious experience, this organic and dynamic process-relational approach did not originate with Whitehead, but finds its roots in the deepest layers of the Judeo-Christian tradition. As with the best of all things in life, the "new" is really the "old," conceived against the backdrop of a changing world. Today's process thinkers find their theological roots in the imagination of the Hebraic "wisdom" tradition, which sees the hand of God in all things large and small, as well as in the "Galilean vision" of divine care and healing for the "least of these."

A process-relational vision of health sees the movement toward health and healing in its diverse religious and secular forms as essentially spiritual in nature. In its response to the need for an integrative vision of health and healing, process thought addresses the following issues: (1) the organic relatedness of all things, (2) the interplay of mind and body, (3) the role of the environment in health, (4) the intersection of technology and values, (5) personal responsibility in health and illness, and (6) the role of God and faith in health and illness. This constructive system provides a fluid Christian vision, which addresses both the symptoms, the model of health, as well as the underlying philosophical causes of the pathology infecting contemporary health care. In so doing, it promotes a vision of wholeness and healing that embraces the totality of our experience, even at the edges of life.

Health and the metaphysics of relationship

In the second and third chapters, we affirmed the significance of a philosophy of relatedness for our personal responses to life-threatening illnesses and for the articulation of a creative and life-supporting image of God. Relationship is essential to reality. In contrast to Descartes' belief that substances, especially the mind and body, are essentially independent and isolated from one another, process thought holds that each drop of experience is constituted by its relationships. Each moment of my life is an act of experience, arising out of my environment and contributing to the world beyond myself. Wholeness is grounded in our ability to embrace our connectedness with the world. Brokenness and sin are related to the inability or refusal to embrace the totality of life.

The world of clear and distinct perceptions and separate and distinct objects, idealized by Descartes and his philosophical followers, is no longer viable for our understanding of reality. Such a world was, of course, always an abstraction. Whereas a world of isolated and independent things leads to a piecemeal and mechanistic vision of humankind and health, a world of interrelated and sympathetic drops of experience leads to an ecological and multidimensional vision of the universe, human existence, and health. In a world of relationships, the body is not understood in terms analogous to a well-made or poorly made clock, but is understood as an intricate organism, a "community of communities" or "society of societies," each intricately connected with the others. A change in one cell has an impact on the whole organism, including the mind and spirit.

In contrast to Newtonian science and its image of independent atoms, modern physics (as well as Whitehead's thought) holds that nature "does not show us any isolated building blocks but rather appears as a complicated web of relations between various parts of a unified whole,"[46] whether that "whole" be an organ, the human body, the planet, or the cosmos. We cannot isolate an organ from its body or a human being from her environment.

This image of the mutual relatedness of all things is reflected in ancient as well as contemporary images of health. Hippocrates, the father of Western medicine, proclaimed that "the well-being of a person is influenced by environmental factors...the quality of air, water and food; the winds and topography and general living habits."[47] The recent definition of health provided by the World Health Organization echoes Hippocrates' "ecological" image of health: health is "the state of complete physical, mental, and social well-being and not merely the absence of disease and infirmity."[48]

This relational image of health is also basic to the Christian understanding of reality. Jesus saw his healing ministry as embracing not only the soul and the body but also the relationship of persons to one another and to the wider economic and political spheres (Luke 4:18–19). Whitehead's metaphysical vision describes these profound insights in terms of the symbiotic relationship of humanity and its environment.

> In fact, the world beyond is so intimately entwined in our natures that unconsciously we identify our more vivid perspectives of it with ourselves. For example, our bodies lie beyond our own individual existence. And yet they are a part of it. We think of ourselves as so intimately entwined in bodily life that man is a complex unity—body and mind. But the body is part of the external world, continuous with it. In fact, it is just as much a part of nature as anything else—a river, a mountain, a cloud. Also, if we are fussily exact, we cannot define where the body begins and nature ends.[49]

The quest for wholeness, accordingly, is grounded in our embrace of our relatedness not only to our friends and family but to the whole universe.

Relatedness, experience, and psychosomatic unity

The current medical model reinforces the experience of separation, isolation, and alienation characteristic of the modern age. Boundaries are sharp between organs or individual persons and their environment. The living and the dying are separated personally as well as physically. The body is often treated as a machine, routinely manipulated by diet, exercise, and sexual technique. Even the positive focus on physical fitness is often pursued apart from consideration of values, emotional well-being, and relationships. In contrast to the ideal of physical health encouraged by athletic contests and advertising agencies, the reality of modern civilization is that the body is often abused by long hours on the job, stress, and improper diet, not to mention eating disorders and substance abuse. Tragically, scant attention has been given to the emotional and spiritual factors that have led to this impasse. Medical practice as well as patient behavior imply that the body can be cared for without consideration of the nonphysical aspects of human life. When this attitude is joined with the materialism and technology characteristic of our time, illness and health alike are addressed in terms of a quick, chemical, surgical, or dietary "fix," apart from any reflection on lifestyle, personal habits, and emotional well-being.

A process-relational approach affirms the psychosomatic unity of life. From this perspective, mind and body—psyche and soma—are essentially related to each other. While mind and body differ quantitatively in terms of richness and complexity of experience, they are similar in kind. The basic units of reality, the momentary "drops of experience" that make up both minds and bodies, are ultimately lively and experiential in nature. The notion of unfeeling matter is an abstraction. There are no dead bodies. Beneath the world of apparently stable and unresponsive objects (i.e., the world of bodies, rocks, tables, and buildings) is a world of microscopic entities, swirling and whirling, arising and perishing, in relationship to one another, in what Fritjof Capra has called the "cosmic dance." We now know that while each drop of experience does not necessarily possess the ability for conscious experience, each created entity—rock, table, book, building, person—is responsive to its local and cosmic environment. Apart from some minimal level of experience, an entity could not relate to God or any other creature. Process thought and the new physics proclaim that the world is lively. The heavens declare the glory of God. The whole earth worships and sings praises to God's name (Psalm 66:1).

In the spirit of the "creation spirituality" of the Bible, process-relational thought proclaims we live in a "psychosomatic" universe, where bodies and minds interpenetrate one another. In a lively universe, God is present not just on the "outside" but "within" each entity's experience as the ultimate source of its creativity and subjectivity. The divine purpose is as fully revealed in the internal purposes of atoms, lilies, sparrows, and the cells of our bodies as it is in the conscious deliberation of humans and nations. My conscious experience of this moment embraces countless, more primitive experiences of the cells constituting my bodily organs, skin, and nervous system. Apart from some form of shared experience, I could neither feel nor have an impact on these more basic bodily components. The

novelty characteristic of conscious experience radiates throughout the body, influencing the immune and cardiovascular systems. Bodily well-being nurtures and supports conscious creativity. Consistent with the nature of the entire universe, health
and illness in human life is always psychosomatic or holistic in
nature. Mind is embodied and body is inspired!

In a dynamic, relational universe, the sources of health and
illness are complex and multifaceted. As Simonton has noted,
the onset of a particular disease cannot be understood in terms
of a single factor, whether it be physical condition, a specific
germ, genetic proclivity, or destructive environmental influences.
The important result of this awareness is the recognition that
one modality of medical treatment cannot fully restore a person
to wholeness. Healing and wholeness require a many-faceted
approach. Spirituality alone cannot fully account for the onset
or remission of a particular illness. If mind, body, and environment interpenetrate one another, then spirituality and emotional
well-being as well as physical fitness and lifestyle are all significant factors in the quality of life and basic life expectancy of
persons. From this perspective, prevention as well as treatment
of illness must be dynamic, multidimensional, and inclusive of
both biomedical and alternative healing techniques.

Cassell, Simonton, and Siegel push us well out into the
frontiers of our relational and holistic universe. But they do not
provide the guidance for the kind of reflection that will help us
integrate their insights with our more traditional Christian belief
systems. We must chart the maps of these frontiers ourselves
by reflecting on our own experiences of health and illness in
light of the biblical tradition and such theological resources as
process-relational thought.

It is clear that our thoughts, emotions, and hopes make a
difference in our physical well-being. Our minds can be both
healers as well as slayers, as Kenneth Pelletier points out. Mainstream Christians have experienced the transforming power of
"positive thinking" and "possibility thinking." At the edges of
Christianity, Science of Mind "treatments" use imaging and
affirmations in order achieve success, health, and peace of mind.
No serious reader of scripture can deny the power of faith in the
healing of bodies as well as minds. The psychosomatic unity of
life is affirmed in Jesus' words to the woman healed of a flow of
blood: "your faith has made you well" (Luke 8:48). Beyond the
doors of mainline churches, practitioners of bioenergetics, rolfing,

reiki, and meditation contend that every thought has a physical counterpart. Just as hopelessness and repressed anger create imbalances to the immune system that may issue in the onset of cancer, so experiences of forgiveness, shared feelings, and hope can unleash previously blocked recuperative forces within the body. Psychologist Lawrence LeShan, whose work has greatly influenced Simonton and Siegel, believes that even persons who have family histories of cancer and heart disease can maintain their well-being through utilizing the healing power of positive spiritual, emotional, and physical images and behaviors.[50]

In my own practice of spiritual counseling, I once encountered a young woman who feared that she would be the next victim in her family's history of breast and ovarian cancer. In the process of our conversations, she discovered that she could respond to her fears by learning to love and affirm her body, especially those organs at risk. Each day, she took time before work to say "I love you" as she looked at herself in the mirror. She learned to meditate and experience God's healing light permeating her body, especially her breasts, uterus, and ovaries. Today, she is no longer a psychological victim of her family's genetic tendencies. Even a cancer-prone personality such as Ivan Ilych can find resources for spiritual, if not physical, healing through a changed perception of himself and his personal history.

Just as emotional and spiritual states are reflected in the body, physical states shape and condition our psychic and emotional experience. In the psychosomatic unity of life, our conscious experience arises from and is greatly conditioned by our bodily state. Accordingly, physical imbalances, such as food allergies and hormonal imbalances, may lead to alterations of psychic well-being. This mind-body continuum is evident in the causes as well as the treatment of "seasonal depressions" that many persons experience. We now recognize that following surgery or the treatment of a broken bone, for example, the experience of health and personal well-being does not return until we once more experience our former confidence in the body and its wholeness. We cannot say that we are fully healed until we can walk and run without the nagging fear of falling. This constant interaction of mind and body makes it ultimately impossible to identify and treat illnesses as merely mental, spiritual, or physical. Health and illness is never "either/or"; it is always "both/and."

Health care, in all of its modes, is most effective when it reflects the multidimensional nature of life. Affirmations, prayer, biofeedback, walking, jogging, swimming, meditation, and regular medical checkups complement, rather than contradict each other. For dying persons, the utilization of meditation and morphine, inspirational reading and alternative diets, pastoral counseling and acupuncture, chemotherapy and the laying on of hands compliment one another as they address the totality of one's physical and spiritual experience. The quest for health involves emphasizing different techniques and approaches at different times of our lives. However, well-being arises from a balanced approach to the spiritual, emotional, relational, physical, and environmental dimensions of life. In a "psychosomatic universe," to neglect the totality of experience, including the presence of God, is not only to go against the nature of the life itself but also to create the psychosomatic imbalances and deficiencies that eventually result in disease.

The ecological vision of health

Human existence is profoundly relational. The interplay of body and mind is merely a manifestation of the interrelatedness of all forms of life.

There are no independent, self-subsistent substances. Rather, the character of any entity reflects the character of its environment. The isolation of humanity from nature, characteristic of the thought of the followers of Descartes and Newton, has been a factor not only in the destruction of the planetary ecosystem, but also in the disastrous denial of environmental factors in health and illness. In spite of Hippocrates' belief that "the well-being of a person is influenced by environmental factors...the quality of air, water, and food; the winds and topography and general living habits,"[51] the biomedical model as well as public opinion has assumed that health and illness can be analyzed and addressed apart from issues of occupation, working conditions, economic situation, and physical environment. The examples of Love Canal, asbestos and lead poisoning, the impact of the recession and unemployment on spouse abuse, as well as studies connecting stress with feelings of powerlessness and insecurity on the job, have demonstrated the significance of the environment in matters of health. Although environmental factors, including family life or contact with carcinogenic substances, are not the only contributors to health or illness, issues of well-being and disease can never be separated from their environmental background.

In his book *Healthy People in Unhealthy Places*, Kenneth Pelletier points out that "all of our attempts at healthy living take place at the periphery of a 40–50 hour block of time work."[52] The cliché, "my job is killing me," is more than a cliché since we encounter a variety of "visible hazards" (toxins, insecticides) as well as "invisible hazards" (noise, crowding, inadequate lighting and ventilation, burnout, instability, lack of communication, boredom) at the workplace.[53] The mechanistic model at the heart of the industrial revolution and early management practices saw the workings of a "clockwork" universe as the model for the work place. In such a universe, workers—like the machinery of a clock—can be treated as purely interchangeable, disposable, and economic parts. However, the everyday problems at work can become a primary source of illness, when there is no corresponding corporate concern for stress reduction, personal growth, and self-affirmation.

In the context of the workplace, Christians must reclaim the historic image of "vocation." From this perspective, work is ultimately a spiritual issue. Our jobs are gifts to God and reflections of our own personal talents. No task in the "body of Christ" is insignificant. Rather, each calling or vocation exists to promote the spiritual well-being of oneself and the community in relationship to God. In this same spirit, nonsectarian movements in organizational development such as "total quality management" affirm the vocational and relational image of employment: workers are provided with task-related opportunities to enhance their sense of meaning, personal value, self-determination, and creativity within a framework of process analysis and continuous improvement. On-site childcare and wellness programs further enhance the quality of the workplace, employee morale, and the relational bonding of families.

Issues of health and illness reach beyond the job and home life. Anxiety, stress, and the loss of hope as well as the experience of well-being are shaped by the quality of the economic, political, and global environment within which persons interact. Personal health is symbiotically related to the health of the biosphere. We cannot survive psychologically or physically if our Mother, the Earth, is perishing. The pervasive fear of ecological destruction, nuclear accidents, ozone depletion, and the overall greenhouse effect challenges our experience of "basic trust" and makes it difficult to commit ourselves to long-term goals. But to be without a vision of the future stifles our imaginations and undermines our immune systems, not to mention the legacy of despair we are passing on to our children. Authentic concern for the holistic welfare of others is reflected in our interest in safe streets, meaningful employment, and economic and medical "safety nets," as well as in personal self-actualization. In a world of relationships there are no impermeable boundaries. The health of the parts and the health of the whole exist in constant interrelatedness.

Nowhere is importance of the environment of health and illness more obvious than in hospitals and nursing homes. While churches have been active in the care of the sick throughout their history, today they must intensify their efforts. In a culture that both fears death and worships technology, the dying are often medically and personally abandoned. Studies have revealed that physicians and nurses tend to make shorter and less frequent visits to dying persons than they do to recovering patients. The uniformity of visiting rules and hospital protocols creates an unhealthy environment for self-affirmation at the edges of life. As an antidote to the dysfunctional character of institutional medicine, the hospice movement has sought to create a healing and growing environment for dying persons and their families. In its emphasis on the family, the hospice movement recognizes that each family is a system whose well-being depends on the interplay of all its members. A significant mental or physical illness upsets the family system's usual balance. While the original state of balance may never be recovered, a new and perhaps more creative family system can be nurtured. An environment that emphasizes self-affirmation, listening, community, and spirituality embodies the Galilean vision that "as you did it to one of the least of these...you did it to me" (Matthew 25:40).

Today, hospitals and nursing homes are challenged to abandon their atomistic and mechanistic approach to medicine and become places of hospitality, which celebrate humanity as well as technology. Today, the hospital is invited to synthesize its tradition of analysis and technical expertise with the affirmation of the importance of the intuitive and unconscious aspects of life in health and illness. Bernie Siegel points out the significance, even to unconscious patients, of conversations held in the operating room. Positive suggestions in the operating room lead not only to less discomfort after surgery but also to earlier discharges from the hospital. With this in mind, Siegel keeps "talking to patients throughout the operation, telling them how things are progressing and enlisting their cooperation if I need it."[54] Siegel points out the importance of the environment to unconscious patients: when a patient's pulse rate is too high during an operation, Siegel has discovered that when he simply tells the unconscious patient, "We'd like your pulse to be 86," for example, the patient's pulse usually goes down to the suggested rate.[55] Accordingly, Siegel suggests that patients can create a healing environment for themselves by playing taped music or affirmations during their operations. From a process-relational perspective, the importance of pastoral calling, phone calls, flowers, and gifts, as well as intercessory prayer and personal touch, can never be underestimated as a force for wholeness at the edges of life.

A process-relational approach to institutional health care inspires a new model of care for the elderly and those with life-threatening illnesses. An emphasis on stimulation, creativity, and imagination would enable the final years of institutionalized patients to be years of generativity rather than boredom. Attuned to possibilities for growth even among persons characterized as senile, health care givers would create environments in which patients could embody their highest level of experience, given their psychological and physical condition.

In the spirit of the apostle Paul, persons with deteriorating physical conditions can nevertheless affirm: "We do not lose heart. Even though our outer nature is wasting away, our inner nature is being renewed day by day" (2 Corinthians 4:16).

A relational and holistic understanding of health and illness challenges us not only to work toward our own personal healing but to cooperate with movements of healing and reconciliation in the workplace, in the home, and in the wider spheres of economics, politics, and ecology. In so doing, we reflect the very nature of the universe itself and become co-creators with God of the processes of life that support and envelop us.

Responsibility and relationship

At the heart of the process-relational, holistic health perspective is the affirmation of personal responsibility in health and illness. Although some "new age" health practitioners imply that illness is the patient's responsibility and creation—and, thus, in their own way, perpetuate the "one cause" idea of health and illness—it is evident, especially from the work of LeShan, Simonton, and Siegel, that we are active participants rather than passive observers in the process of health and illness. It is well known, even within the medical community, that diseases such as arthritis, asthma, colitis, heart disease, and ulcers are related to a person's lifestyle, conscious or unconscious feelings, and perception of reality. The "benefits" of illness are also well known: illness allows persons not only to avoid unpleasant situations but also to rest and receive the care and attention they are often unable to request for themselves in any other way.

I believe that each person has a role, conscious or unconscious, in his susceptibility to illness; and each person also has a role in her recovery and return to wholeness. Through self-reflection, we can come to realize how our values and emotional lives have contributed to our susceptibility to illness. We can also discover that, despite our past behavior and present experience, transformation is always possible. The possibility of transformation, however, rests on the recognition that each moment is an intersection of repetition and newness, of fate and freedom. Each moment is a center of decision making and creativity as well as an opportunity to cooperate with God's aim toward healing. Obedience to God's will, or aim, is synonymous with growth in personal responsibility, freedom, and relatedness.

The process-relational vision of health encourages personal participation in every aspect of life, including health care. While the search for causes is essential for diagnosis, the quest for responsibility is just as essential for prevention and treatment. From a process-relational perspective, the explicit or implicit encouragement of passivity or blind obedience to authority figures goes against the very nature of the universe and our own deepest nature. God calls us to be partners not only in the divine adventure but in the adventures of our own lives and relationships. In its affirmation of freedom and responsibility, process-relational thought affirms the apostle Paul's admonition: "Don't let the world around you squeeze you into its own mold" (Romans 12:2, Phillips). Accordingly, issues such as aging or life-expectancy are not absolutes. Our expectations for our lives are not governed by statistics and cultural norms but are related to our desire and ability to accept responsibility for our creative response to the events of our lives. The inherent creativity of persons should lead us to encourage our physicians and other healers to become fellow companions and teachers rather than authority figures. Our mutual task is one of partnership, adventure, and persuasion. In the context of authentic relationships and mutual respect, the role of the physician, or other healers, is to facilitate our exploration of those possibilities that encourage wholeness and beauty of experience. Such responses by our healers, or healing companions, are acts of trust in the healing forces of the universe and recognitions of each person's "center" of self-creation. Healing is a social process.

In his reflections on the psychotherapeutic response to persons with cancer, Lawrence LeShan affirms the centrality of creativity and responsibility in the healing process in maintaining that "the central task of psychology...is celebrating the full individuality of the patient."[56] Even with those persons living with life-threatening illness, creativity is possible as it relates to "the expansion, growth, and freeing of the self rather than physical recovery."[57] Even as our physical health deteriorates, we may grow in openness to God and other persons. Illness provides an opportunity, within limits of our condition, for self-creativity and personal transformation. We are challenged to explore the potential for healing and beauty of experience even in the context of illness. For Simonton, Siegel, and LeShan, meditation, imagination, and self-affirmation are the tools by which even persons with life-threatening illnesses may move from despair, fatalism, and victimization to freedom, creativity, and empowerment. As Christians, we might add to this list of creative tools such practices as prayer, confession and forgiveness of sin, and the use of the imagination in the study of scripture. Relationship and responsibility are intricately related insofar as the more we embrace the connectedness of the world, including our bodies, the more we discern the limits as well as the possibilities for exploration and generativity in the creation of our experience.

Values and technology in health and illness

Modern medicine and the orientation toward fitness in our time has centered on the body as the primary, if not the sole, focus of health and illness. In the practice of biomedicine, it has been assumed that authentic health care can be understood only in terms of objectively quantifiable and observable data. Accordingly, health care delivery is seen primarily as a matter of adequate technological care rather than preventive medicine. While this empirical approach has been a major factor in the detection as well as the surgical and chemical response to dis-

ease, it has typically neglected questions of values, ethical decision making, and patient interests. When Dr. N. declares to
Simone that "I am doing what has to be done," he is proclaiming the sovereignty of medical technology over personal and
spiritual values. Yet, the failure of biomedicine to consider non-
objective issues such as emotions, subjectivity, intuition, and
spiritual insight has left in its wake the seemingly unsurmountable
ethical issues that face medicine today.

A worldview that envisages the cosmos as mechanical and
the body as a machine to be manipulated eventually comes to
see human existence itself as objective and mechanical. The
assumption that the body and the natural world are essentially
valueless and nonresponsive results in a philosophy and technology that make questions of human values insignificant or
superfluous. In contrast, a vision of reality that proclaims the
universality of experience and the reality of relatedness results
in a recognition and respect for the value and experience present
in all things. In such a universe, subjectivity, decision making,
and value are omnipresent.

If experience, value, and relationship characterize everything that exists, questions of health care and medicine are also
questions of values and ethics as well as objectivity and technology. There is no purely objective medicine. An authentic
understanding of reality inspires a health care system that affirms the values of patients and health care givers alike. In
cases of long-term care, personal values may be as compelling
as technological options. This is especially evident in the care
of dying persons. At the edges of physical existence, technological issues recede into the background. While hygiene, comfort, and pain relief are essential to the care of the dying, the
primary issues for conscious patients revolve around how the
person wishes to live out her or his remaining days both in
terms of treatment and environment. Even unconscious patients
must be treated as if in some fundamental way they, too, are
interested in the spiritual aspects of their well-being. If issues of
values are basic to reality, then questions of values and spirituality are as important as issues of technological care.

A concern for values also inspires treatment programs that
are collegial and nonhierarchical in nature. Physicians, nurses,
and other healing companions are challenged to respect the
value concerns of those whom they treat. As a guide to health
care planning, persons should be provided with resources that

will enable them to engage in reflection on their values and ethics with their own health care givers. In the development and use of new technologies, we must consider what is beneficial not only to ourselves but also to our community and to the ecosphere.

On the flip side of the coin, while the point of health care is the well-being of patients, the emotional and spiritual needs of physicians, nurses, and other healing companions must also be considered as essential to the healing process. The training implications are, of course, massive. Educated to revere objectivity, detachment, and technological expertise above all else, many physicians are often unable to deal creatively with their own feelings about death, failure, stress, and perfectionism. In spite of Cassell's reminder that the physician as person is one of the greatest tools of healing, most physicians forget the significance of their own healing power as persons and their constant need to replenish their own spiritual and moral energy. When the values, ethics, and personal concerns of a physician or nurse are neglected, the eventual result is illness, substance abuse, burnout, and the death of the healing spirit. The physician who respects her own experience and values, who trusts subjectivity as well as objectivity, and aids in healing with gentle touch and empathetic words as well as surgery and medication is, indeed, a "wounded healer" whose contact with the pain and joy of life becomes the healing balm for the vulnerable and broken who seek her care.

The ultimate frame of reference for healing and medicine

Our vision of reality shapes not only what we see but how we respond to our life's events. The dualistic and mechanistic orientation characteristic of our culture has placed issues of God and spirituality at the edges of life not only institutionally but also personally. Where the heavens once declared the glory of God to our parents, now the heavens are silent to many persons in our time. Humanity is alone, isolated and without companionship in an essentially valueless and indifferent universe. As philosopher Bertrand Russell points out:

> That man is the product of causes which had no prevision of the ends they were achieving; that his origin, his growth, his hopes and fears, his loves and his beliefs are but the outcome of accidental collocations of atoms....that the

labor of all the ages, all the direction, all the inspiration, all the noonday brightness of human genius, are destined to extinction in the vast death of the solar system, and that the whole of man's achievement must inevitably be buried beneath the debris of a universe in ruins—all these things, if not quite beyond dispute, are...nearly certain....Brief and powerless is man's life; on him and all his race the slow, sure doom falls pitiless and dark. Blind to good and evil, reckless of destruction, omnipotent matter rolls in its relentless way.[58]

This essentially tragic vision of life is portrayed by Nobel Prize winner Steven Weinberg, who claims that despite the beauty of the earth, "we live in an overwhelmingly hostile universe...the more the universe seems comprehensible, the more it seems pointless."[59] In an absurd and tragic universe in which death is the ultimate end of our efforts, it is only appropriate that institutional medicine and our own personal responses to illness be characterized by fearful clinging to bodily existence. An aimless and mechanistic vision of reality inspires a negative, illness-oriented medicine as well as sense of hopelessness at the edges of life. Chaos and entropy assail us at every side, and when we call out for aid the universe remains silent. Ironically, the vision of reality at the base of modern medicine reflects the causes of its most feared disease: the macrocosm mirrors the cold, mechanical, and uncaring world identified with the cancer-prone person.

In spite of the materialist's claims, however, we hunger for meaning and companionship at the edges of life. We yearn for a world in which chaos and entropy are balanced by a force that promotes order, beauty, and wholeness. Although surveys suggest that most Americans believe God exists, few are able to integrate that belief with issues of health, vocation, lifestyle, and spirituality. Nevertheless, in moments of grief and illness, we discover unexpected and surprising resources for healing, comfort, and new life, which cannot be attributed to the motions of "blind and omnipotent matter."

In the Christian tradition, this counterforce to suffering, meaninglessness, and chaos has been traditionally called "God." But if Christian faith is to become a significant factor in the quest for health and healing, we must rethink and reformulate our traditional images of God. Our vision of God, like our vision of reality and human existence, makes a difference in health and illness. This fact is obvious, for example, in the healings attributed to the laying on of hands and intercessory prayer. It is equally obvious that images of God may be factors in the susceptibility to illness; for example, feelings of guilt and punishment play a role in the onset of illness as well as in hindering the effectiveness of medical treatment. In the case of Christian Science, an image of God may even prevent a parent from seeking lifesaving medical care for her child. As William James wisely noted, our beliefs have practical consequences. Prayer, the laying on of hands, and the Lord's Supper are powerful not merely because of the healing power inherent in their practice but also as a result of the trust and expectation they evoke. In a process-relational universe we can affirm, on the one hand, "that your faith has made you whole" and, on the other, that "your faith has made you ill." Our personal quest, accordingly, must be to explore creative and life-enhancing images of God as they relate to health and illness.

The exclusion of issues of God and spirituality from health and illness has resulted, as I have maintained, from the assumptions of a mechanistic and dualistic worldview. It is also a result of a negative and life-denying theology whose identification of illness entirely with sin or the will of God has alienated many persons who have sought comfort from the church. If illness is viewed as the punishment of sin, then the patient deserves whatever befalls her. As some conservative Christians point out, AIDS is God's punishment of America for its immorality. Ironically, America's materialism and sinfulness were cited as the primary cause of the great cholera epidemic of the 1830s! In those days, persons with cholera carried the moral stigma that persons with AIDS do today. When illness is seen as the will of an immutable and all-determining God, then fighting against illness is contrary to the will of God. Further, if God's perfect and immutable law is violated by certain customary medical practices, then it is better for the believer to die than to receive treatment—if, for example, saving the body by means of a blood transfusion brings condemnation on the soul.

Contemporary medicine and theological reflection have rightly challenged those images of God that have seen illness and pain as a result of God's will or the execution of God's judgment. We must also question the logic of a faith that would sacrifice human well-being to literalistic interpretations of divine law. Tragically, the clash of religion and medicine has often reflected a religious viewpoint that was itself mechanistic, rigid, and heartless and, seemingly, unconcerned about any values other than the glorification of abstract biblical principles. When the Galilean vision is forgotten, Christianity itself becomes an instrument of death and destruction to persons at the edges of life.

In contrast to these destructive and life-denying images of God, a process-relational vision of God is not only positive and life-affirming but also affirmative of the practice of medicine in its many forms. Within every drop of experience and the universe as a whole, the same omnipresent force aims at wholeness, beauty, and complexity. Beneath the apparent entropy and chaos of existence is a community of shared experience that reveals an active principle urging the created world toward the realization of its highest possible ideals. Empathy and cooperation are prior to, and more basic than, competition or the survival of the fittest. While evil, injustice, sickness, and entropy are real, they are balanced by forces of order, complexity, novelty, love, and beauty, which Christian faith has identified with the presence of God in the world. Accordingly, wherever there is healing, even when the names of God and Christ are not invoked, God is its ultimate source.

In chapters two and three, I explored the possibility of growth at the edges of life and pointed to the role of God in human experience. I suggested that divine power is most appropriately understood in terms of relationship, passion, and empathy. I believe that illness is never a manifestation of God's will or a punishment of self-destructive behavior. Guidance and transformation, rather than judgment, reflect God's presence in human brokenness. Within moments of judgment and confession, God is present as the voice of growth, reconciliation, hope, and forgiveness.

Whereas traditional images of God focus on divine omnipotence, process-relational thought maintains that in any experience, even those of illness, God is but one of the factors. Genuine freedom, as well as contingency, exists even in a world that reflects, at every level, the presence of a creative and caring God. In God's quest for beauty and wholeness, God does not violate the laws of nature. Rather, God works creatively within the context of the world and its dynamic interplay of order and chaos. Accordingly, God's presence is unobtrusive and often indiscernible. Nevertheless, God's presence makes a difference in health and illness. In each moment of our lives, God seeks the highest realization of beauty and value. Although we as individuals may be oblivious to the divine presence, our ignorance does not negate the divine impact in our lives. As I will suggest in the next chapter, awareness of God's presence releases creative energies from which the experience of personal and spiritual wholeness arises. These moments of gradual or spontaneous healing are not, however, disruptions of the laws of nature, but rather are explicit manifestations of the implicit and otherwise inobtrusive divine energy present in all things. Our openness to the transformative energy of the divine—that is, our faith—is the source of the courage to initiate new behaviors, to imagine new possibilities, to express love and anger, and to discover undreamed of resources for healing and change.

Process-relational thought proclaims a "personal" and "connected" universe, in which beauty and value make a difference. Freed from the bondage of isolation, we are invited to experience the universe as supportive and hospitable. The healing companion does not fight alone; the whole universe supports her and her patient's efforts at healing. Indeed, far from revealing a heartless universe, our body's own immune and recuperative systems reveal an inner movement toward health and beauty. The health care giver and his patient can relax and trust the processes of healing within the life of the patient as well as the health care giver. Accordingly, the role of the physician is to cooperate and facilitate the patient's experience of the healing energies residing in the patient, the physician, and the treatment itself.

In a relational universe, God is concerned with our bodies as well as our souls. Wherever there is a movement toward healing, God is present. Accordingly, medicine and theology support one another. The incarnation of God in all things is an invitation to explore new and powerful dimensions of experience as they operate within the healing process. In the following chapter I will consider these hidden sources of healing revealed in the dynamic and often forgotten interplay of spiritual healing, medicine, and mortality.

Notes

[1]Simone de Beauvoir, *A Very Easy Death* (New York: Warner Books, 1973), p. 34.
[2]*Ibid.*, p. 25.
[3]*Ibid.*, p. 33.

[4]*Ibid.*, p. 37.

[5]*Ibid.*, p. 34.

[6]Eric Cassell, *The Healer's Art* (Philadelphia: J.P. Lippencott, 1976), p. 182.

[7]William F. May, *The Physician's Covenant* (Philadelphia: Westminster Press, 1983), p. 31.

[8]*Ibid.*, p. 34.

[9]George Engel, "The Need for a New Medical Model: A Challenge for Biomedicine," *Science* 196:4286 (April 8, 1977), p. 129.

[10]*Ibid.*, p. 130.

[11]Paul Ramsey, "On (Only) Caring for the Dying," in Robert Weir, *Ethical Issues in Death and Dying* (New York: Columbia University Press, 1974), p. 213.

[12]Cassell, *The Healer's Art*, p. 15.

[13]*Ibid.*, p. 87.

[14]*Ibid.*, p. 200.

[15]*Ibid.*

[16]*Ibid.*, p. 204.

[17]*Ibid.*, p. 210.

[18]*Ibid.*

[19]*Ibid.*, p. 114.

[20]Robert Chernin Cantor, *And a Time to Live* (New York: Harper and Row, 1978), p. 9.

[21]*Ibid.*, p. 22.

[22]*Ibid.*, p. 32.

[23]O. Carl Simonton, Stephanie Matthews Simonton, James Creighton, *Getting Well Again* (Los Angeles: J.P. Tarcher, 1978), p. 4.

[24]*Ibid.*, p. 10.

[25]*Ibid.*, p. 38.

[26]*Ibid.*, p. 51.

[27]*Ibid.*, pp. 68-70.

[28]*Ibid.*, p. 31f.

[29]*Ibid.*, p. 78.

[30]*Ibid.*, p. 77.

[31]*Ibid.*, p. 7.

[32]*Ibid.*, p. 8.

[33]Bernie Siegel, *Love, Medicine, and Miracles* (New York: Harper and Row, 1986), p. 180.

[34]Bernie Siegel, *Peace, Love, and Healing* (New York: Harper and Row, 1989), p. 16.

[35]*Ibid.*, p. 36.

[36]*Ibid.*

[37]Siegel, *Love, Medicine, and Miracles*, p. 156.

[38]Paul Tillich, *The Meaning of Health* (Chicago: Exploration Press, 1984), p. 16.

[39]*Ibid.*, p. 17.

[40]*Ibid.*, p. 167f.

[41]*Ibid.*, p. 172.

[42]*Ibid.*

[43]*Ibid.*

[44]*Ibid.*, p. 173.

[45]Tillich, *Systematic Theology*, Volume 3, p. 282.

[46]Fritjof Capra, *The Turning Point* (New York: Bantam, 1983), p. 81.

[47]Quoted in M. Todd, "The Challenge to Medicine: Prevention of Illness," in E.M. Goldway, editor, *Inner Balance: The Power of Holistic Healing* (Englewood Cliffs, N.J.: Prentice-Hall, 1979), p. 2.

[48]*Ibid.*, p. 3.

[49]Whitehead, *Modes of Thought*, p. 21.

[50]Lawrence LeShan, *You Can Fight for Your Life* (New York: M. Evans and Company, 1977), p. 12.

[51]E.M. Goldway, *Inner Balance: The Power of Holistic Healing*, (Englewood Cliffs, N.J.: Prentice-Hall, p. 2.

[52]Kenneth Pelletier, *Healthy People in Unhealthy Places: Stress and Fitness at Work* (New York: Delacorte, 1984), p. 1.

[53]*Ibid.*, p. 3.

[54]Bernie Siegel, *Peace, Love, and Healing*, p. 94f.

[55]*Ibid.*, p. 95.

[56]LeShan, *You Can Fight for Your Life*, p. 35.

[57]*Ibid.*, p. 96.

[58]Bertrand Russell, *A Free Man's Worship and Other Essays* (London: George Allen and Unwin, LTD., 1976), p. 10.

[59]Steven Weinberg, *The First Three Minutes* (New York: Basic Books, 1977), p. 144.

5

Christian Theology and the Recovery of Healing

Exploring the Frontiers of Healing

New images of health and wholeness invite us to explore the edges of our known world without being afraid of experiencing novel and surprising powers and forces. As we explore the frontiers of health and healing, we reenact an adventure much like that of the "middle-aged Square" described in Edwin Abbot's fantasy *Flatland*. As the story opens, a middle-aged Square has a disturbing dream in which he visits the one-dimensional realm of Lineland and attempts to share his experience of two dimensions with one of its residents. What seems self-evident to him, the perception of a two-dimensional world, is unbelievable in Lineland. He awakens from his dream just as the Linelanders are about to attack him for his false and socially destructive opinions. Later that day, as he attempts to help his grandson with his mathematical studies, his grandson speculates on the possibility of a third dimension. The Square proclaims the notion absurd and impossible and fears that his grandson's attitude will ill-prepare him to meet the demands of two-dimensional reality.

111

Yet, that very night, the Square has a life-transforming encounter: he is visited by an inhabitant of the three-dimensional world of Spaceland. The world his spherical visitor describes violates the vision of reality by which the Square has always lived. Realizing that argument alone will not convince the Square of the existence of three dimensions, the Sphere creates for him an experience of depth. Amid the dizzying and shattering confusion of three dimensions, the Square exclaims, "Either this is madness or this is hell." "It is neither," replies the Sphere, "It is knowledge; it is three dimensions. Open your eyes once again and try to look steadily."[1] Caught up in the ecstasy of this newly discovered dimension, the Square baffles even his own spherical guide by suggesting the possibility of unseen dimensions beyond the third.

The process-relational invitation to a holistic vision of the human adventure opens us to a multidimensional reality. The experience of these new dimensions of reality is both shattering and transforming. Like the cartographers of old who had to revise their maps of the world following the voyages of Columbus, we are challenged by the new visions of the relationship of body, mind, and spirit to revise our own understandings of human existence and its cosmic environment. The truly religious quest for healing and human wholeness proclaims that reality is deeper and more surprising than we had imagined. But like the middle-aged Square, we are often content to dwell in the comfortable and well-mapped world of everyday, limited sense-experience.

I believe that this complacency and metaphysical conservativism is evident in the predominant attitude of Christians toward the healing ministry of Jesus Christ. Although moe than one-fifth of the gospel accounts of Jesus' ministry involve healing, the concern for physical healing has been relegated to the fringes of the church. On the one hand, the church has traditionally maintained that the primary concern of individuals should be the salvation of their eternal souls. On the other hand, following the influence of Isaac Newton, the church has also affirmed a strict cause and effect understanding of physical reality, which limited the scope of reality to what we can verify with our five senses. On the whole, whether traditionalist or evangelical, fundamentalist or liberal, the "center channel" of church leadership has shared the common belief that the territory of faith belongs primarily to issues of personal devotion and individual responsibility. Concern for wholeness of body and spirit has remained at the periphery of faith.

In recent years, liberal Christianity and liberation theology have appropriately reclaimed the biblical awareness that authentic faith must concern itself with issues of corporate justice and morality. However, in light of the crises of hunger, economic injustice, and apartheid, many such theologians have contended that the concern for personal healing and spiritual growth is the privilege of an upper-class mentality, which often uses the quest for wholeness of mind and body as a distraction from the more fundamental issues of political justice and social responsibility. But an "either-or" understanding of personal healing and social justice is not necessary. All healing, whether it be political or physical, spiritual or economic, is a reflection of God's presence in our world. Today, the work of faith communities such as Sojourners and the Church of the Savior in Washington, D.C., witnesses to the interdependence of social justice, personal spirituality, and holistic health care in the authentic expression of Christian faith.

The essential link between spirituality and liberation—or, to phrase it another way, the healing of the person and the healing of the planet—is seldom discerned within our churches. Nevertheless, the biblical witness to a holistic spirituality (for example, Luke 4:18–19) is strong to those who have ears to hear and eyes to see it. Thankfully, within mainstream Christianity a growing number of spiritual adventurers are beginning to seek those mysterious revelatory dimensions of reality hidden within and beneath the experiences of our five senses and their companion, human reason.

But Christian leadership, especially theologians and clergy, has unfortunately lagged far behind "secular" psychologists, nurses, physicists, and even physicians in their reflections on the exciting relationship between healing and illness. Dramatic healings and spontaneous remissions are recorded even within the hospital setting. Yet they are often ignored because they make no sense within the closed-system world of Newtonian physics. Miracles or unexpected healings are ruled out because they do not conform to our understanding of reality or religious experience. They are seen as violations of the laws of nature or evidence of a prior, undetected, "psychosomatic" (here, seen as a pejorative term) ailment.

Still, miracles do continue to occur—at mass healing services and revivals, in meetings with Christian Science practitioners, and in "new age" communities utilizing crystals, "channeled" readings, and healing touch. Mainstream Christians as well as Newtonian physicians are baffled and threatened by the powers attributed to the Christian and non-Christian laying on of hands, crystals, bodywork therapies, prayer, guided imaging, and meditation. Despite mainstream Christianity's uneasiness, interest in healing and mysticism, especially among laypersons, has increased in the last decade. Christians are exploring the healing dimensions of their faith: sacramental churches (such as Roman Catholic and Episcopal) and traditionally liberal churches (such as the United Church of Christ and United Methodist Church) are seeking to revive and incorporate traditional healing rituals such as the "laying on of hands," "anointing with oil," and intercessory prayer in the context of liturgical services. My own experience as a professor in an adult education program associated with Wesley Theological Seminary in Washington, D.C., has led me to believe that, within mainline churches, a growing number of laypersons have had paranormal and healing experiences but feel uncomfortable in sharing them with their pastors.

Some Christians are affirming that Jesus is the spiritual father of medicine. Various religious groups have responded to the AIDS crisis by a combination of healing touch, body massage, and personal support. However, little theological reflection on healing has occurred within mainstream Christianity.[2] Like the culture that surrounds it, mainstream Christianity has been stifled by its unimaginative adherence to outmoded, dualistic, and unhelpful views of God and the world. Today, Christian faith is in need of new theological images to serve as the basis for a practical theology of healing.

Process-relational theology provides fertile ground for the integration of spirituality and healing within the church. My theological approach to healing is grounded in an affirmation of medicine and natural law as well as the dynamic presence of God. It finds its foundation in the metaphysics of health and illness articulated in the previous chapter. In this chapter, I wish to explore the frontiers of health and healing by considering (1) the primary streams of spiritual healing in the past century, exemplified by the healing ministries of Christian Science and mainstream healers such as Agnes Sanford and Ambrose and

Olga Worrall; (2) the new models of healing found in therapeutic touch, bodywork therapies, and the laying on of hands; and (3) the resources of process-relational thought as foundations for a theology of healing. I believe that an adequate theology of healing must affirm both the continuity of all healing experiences (that is, the same universal principles relate to both gradual and spontaneous healings and medical and religious healings) and the vital combination of God's love and human faith in the process of healing. Further, an adequate theology of healing must explain the interplay of healing and natural law as it explores the possibility of realities lying beyond ordinary sense experience. Philosophically and personally, it is clear to me that physical healing must reflect rather than violate the intricate and dynamic web of life. Finally, a theology of healing must provide an explanation for "failures" in the healing process as well as affirming the deeper possibilities of personal and holistic healing.

Healing and Christianity: Christian Science and Spiritual Healing

In 1879 a small group of evangelical New Englanders, under the leadership of Mary Baker Eddy, voted to "organize a church designed to commemorate the word and works of our Master, which reinstate positive Christianity and its lost element of healing."[3] As a result of the healing powers released by an experience of spiritual illumination, the group's leader, Mary Baker Eddy, had been healed of an illness that had left her bed-ridden, in great pain, and with little hope of recovery. She interpreted her startling recovery as a manifestation of the divine law that Spirit alone is real. This life-changing event marked the birth of Christian Science. Since that time thousands of persons have found healing through the ministry of Mary Baker Eddy and her followers.

According to Christian Science and all "New Thought" groups (e.g, Science of Mind and the Church of Religious Science), to know the truth of reality is to experience freedom from sickness, sin, evil, and death. To dwell in the realm of illusion and falsehood is to become a prisoner of the forces of death and destruction. Healing and illness are grounded in one's metaphysical vision.

As the most radical of the "New Thought" movements, Christian Science affirms a monistic metaphysics of the spirit: the world is spiritual in nature. God is Spirit and is, accordingly, the unchanging fountain of goodness and health. Only the eternal, perfect, and unchanging is real. The everchanging, imperfect, and perishing world of the senses is an illusion, alien to the Divine Mind. "Theology and physics," Mrs. Eddy wrote, "tell us that both Spirit and matter are real and good, whereas the fact is that Spirit is good and matter is Spirit's opposite."[4] In her reflections on the reality of mind and illusion of matter, Mrs. Eddy maintained:

> There is no life, truth, intelligence, nor substance in matter. All is infinite Mind and its infinite manifestation, for God is All-in-all. Spirit is immortal Truth, matter is mortal error. Spirit is real and eternal; matter is unreal and temporal. Spirit is God, and man is His image and likeness. Therefore man is not material; he is spiritual.[5]

The physical world is an illusion, created by mortal mind's adherence to falsehood. "Matter is an error of statement ....Nothing we can say or believe regarding matter is immortal, for matter is temporal and is therefore a mortal phenomenon, a human concept, sometimes beautiful, always erroneous."[6] Truth and reality apply only to changeless Spirit. All else is an illusion that leads to separation, sin, and sickness. Even our most obvious physical experiences, those pertaining to illness and pain, are human concepts with no basis in reality. "You say a boil is painful; but that is impossible, for matter without mind is not painful. The boil simply manifests, through inflammation and swelling, a belief in pain, and this belief is called a boil."[7] Belief produces disease and all its symptoms. Even apparently neutral phenomena such as bones have substance only because of our belief in them. "They are phenomena of the mind of mortals....formed first [in the mind of the child] by the parent's mind, through self-division."[8] Even death is an illusion, for "man is immortal and the body cannot die, because matter has no life to surrender. The human concepts named matter, death, disease, sickness, and sin are all that can be destroyed."[9] Death is merely a dream from which the sleeper is to be awakened. "Man is the same after as before a broken bone or the body guillotined."[10]

While such an extremist view may sound absurd to the average mainline Christian, it serves us to note the fact that Christian Science represents the logical opposite pole to the model of reality presented by contemporary biomedicine. Whereas the biomedical model sees illness and recovery only in terms of bodily existence, Christian Science sees these same realities as entirely spiritual in nature. According to Christian Science theologian Robert Peel, even the insights of holistic medicine "fall short of the healing offered by Christian healing that relies wholly on spiritual means."[11] According to Christian Science, matter has neither causality nor reality. Illness and death result only from unenlightened mental concepts. The treatment of illness requires only the process of awakening the mind to its true reality as a manifestation of the Divine Mind.

For Christian Science, unlike Religious Science or other "New Thought" movements, there is no place at all for physical medicine in healing, since the effects of medical care themselves are solely the result of the faith we place in them. "Material medicine substitutes drugs for the power of God—even the might of Mind—to heal the body....truth divests material drugs of their imaginary power."[12] In this extreme view, although the use of drugs may seem helpful, it is, in fact, evil because drugs prevent persons from relying on God alone for healing.[13] Since disease is purely a manifestation, or externalization, of false thinking, it is cured only by a return to the truth.

What mainline Christians can learn from Christian Science and other "New Thought" churches is the importance of reminding the sick that they are not helpless victims. At the onset of illness, or even more ideally in a preventive fashion, lessons need to be taught; individual consciousness needs to be "raised" about the power of our belief systems and their effect on our health. This should be an important focus of our weekly church school teaching as well as the counseling of elders and ministers. In Christian Science, the reading of scripture or *Science and Health* combined with the faith of the practitioner and patient serves as a catalyst that opens the patient to the reality of God and the unreality of illness and death. Their Christianity is therefore "science" insofar as it awakens persons to the immutable laws of God, the laws of Spirit that lie beneath the changing phenomena of the material world.

Despite the controversy that has surrounded Christian Science when it has involved the death of a child due to withholding of normal medical care, it is clear that the "fruits" of Christian Science have been borne out by countless healings of spirit and body. The more moderate "New Thought" (Religious Science, Unity, Science of Mind) churches that make no official rulings about the exclusion of customary medical care are a profound testimony to the reality of faith in God in the healing process. I have lifted up the Christian Science alternative because of its extremism, which, like the biomedical model, errs more in what it denies than in what it affirms. While the biomedical model exaggerates the power of physical technology, Christian Science exaggerates the power of mind. A more moderate blend of these two extremes is called for. While it is true that the mind is powerful and that openness to the God releases the everpresent forces of liberation and wholeness, the power of God and the human spirit are inextricably related to the world of bodies and must work within physical as well as spiritual law. The notable failures and fatalities attributed to Christian Science are the result of its denial of the physical world and the consequent failure to employ its resources.

Accordingly, the primary issue between a holistic Christian perspective and Christian Science is their respective understandings of the body and the physical world in health and healing. Whereas Christian Science maintains that value and being pertain only to that which is eternal, unchanging, and spiritual, a process-relational vision of reality holds that wherever there is existence, there is value. Therefore, that which is temporal and changing and embodied also reflects the beauty and goodness of God. An adequate and inclusive vision of health must take into account our primitive intuitions of physical existence, provided by our bodies, and the wisdom of our body in relationship to the mind and the spirit. In a process-relational Christian perspective, mind, body, and spirit are one, but they are one in a vital, open, and growing relationship with one another. I believe that the healing of the whole person must involve the interplay of the mind, body, and spirit, each of which alone is a vital but not all-encompassing element in the healing process.

Healing in Mainstream Christianity: Agnes Sanford and Olga and Ambrose Worrall

While the theology and practice of Christian Science and New Thought lie at the fringes of traditional Christianity, the healing practice of Agnes Sanford, Ambrose Worrall, and Olga Worrall lies in the center channel of mainstream Christianity.

The work of Sanford and the Worralls serves as a reminder that healing is not just the possession of New Thought, the "new age," or the charismatic churches, but also flourishes in sacramental and liturgical churches. The testimony of the Worralls and Sanford is all the more remarkable insofar as they were laypersons who practiced their healing ministry in the context of their daily occupations. Ambrose Worrall was an engineer. Olga Worrall was a homemaker who established healing ministries in Methodist churches in Baltimore, Maryland. Agnes Sanford was a lay volunteer, a mother, and the spouse of an Episcopalian rector, and became a healing colleague of Morton Kelsey, one of the best known and most insightful adventurers at the edges of Christian healing and spirituality.

The ministry of Sanford and the Worralls is grounded in a vision of reality that affirms that God's healing energy is everpresent and ever-active. In Agnes Sanford's understanding, the whole universe is full of the creative energy of God.[14] In contrast to the Newtonian vision of lifeless and unconnected matter, Sanford maintains that the body is an energetic vehicle through which divine energy, like electricity, flows.[15] In contrast to Christian Science, the healing ministries of Sanford and the Worralls affirm the reality and significance of the body in human wholeness. Indeed, the possibility of healing rests on the divine affirmation of and embodiment within physical existence. When we understand the divine laws of nature, we can "speed up the natural healing of the body."[16] The beauty of this approach rests in the belief that wherever healing is present, be it by laying on of hands, chemotherapy, or surgery, God is also present. Divine energy is a loving vibration flowing through all things. As Ambrose Worrall states, the "doctor and medicine are also instruments of divine healing."[17] Neither Sanford nor the Worralls worked as healers, or healing companions, with persons who refused to see physicians.

We are surrounded by a divine energy field. As Agnes Sanford proclaims, "God's light shines in me continually."[18] Openness to this divine and creative energy brings health and wholeness. We may insulate or deplete this energy through negativity or overextension. Just as we can consciously or unconsciously block ourselves off to this energy, we can consciously open to it through disciplines of spiritual awareness. We can also receive this energy as a "gift" from others who radiate it to us. In this context, the "healer's" role is to open herself to God's healing energy and thus become a channel radiating divine energy to the person seeking her assistance. One need not be a contemplative or mystic to do this. A doctor, nurse, pastor, or lay caregiver can be intentionally open to this divine energy through disciplines of spiritual awareness.

By opening to God through imagination, meditation, and prayer, the healing companion can become an especially "wide" channel for God's healing energy, which helps the healing energies within the person being treated to activate and align himself with the divine energy in all things. Agnes Sanford recalls the following experience of a little girl suffering from infantile paralysis:

> One day I placed my hands above the rigid knee in the instinctive laying on of hands that every mother knows....I asked that the light of God might shine through me into the small, stiff knee and make it well. "Oh, take your hands away!" cried the little girl. "It's hot."
>
> "That's God's power working in your knee, Sally," I replied. "It's like electricity working in your lamp. I guess it has to be hot to make the knee come back to life. So you just stand it now for a few minutes, while I tell you about Peter Rabbit....
>
> "Now crawl out to the edge of the bed, Sally, and see if that leg will bend," I directed the child. She pulled herself to the edge of the bed and sat up. And the leg that had been rigid, bent at an angle of forty-five degrees. Within two weeks she was walking.[19]

Whether by the laying on of hands or facilitating the imagination and faith of the patient, spiritual healing within the mainstream Christian tradition seeks to embrace and channel the healing energies of God. In a world permeated by divine energy, a world in which spiritual energy resides in every cell, there is no dichotomy of sacred and secular or mind and body. Healing is not a violation of the laws of nature but a reflection of the deepest energies within all things. The Christian healing, advocated by Sanford and the Worralls, can take place anywhere: in liturgical healing services, through intercessory prayer, or through one-to-one encounters.

Healing the Energy Field:
Usui, Brennan, and Krieger

The healing ministries of Agnes Sanford and the Worralls seek to mediate God's energy to persons in need. The same quest for God's healing presence was the catalyst that inspired the discovery of the *reiki* (universal or divine energy) form of touch healing. In the late nineteenth century Mikao Usui was the rector of Doshisha University in Kyoto, Japan. Usui, a Christian minister, received the call to a healing ministry when one of his students startled him by asking, "Do you believe the Bible is literally true?" When Usui responded in the affirmative, the student asked him to perform a miracle just as Jesus did. Usui's search for the answer took him to America, where he studied Christianity and comparative religions, and back to Japan where he studied Buddhism. Still unable to find the answer, Usui retreated to a mountaintop outside of Kyoto where he meditated for twenty-one days. On the last day, Usui experienced a light coming toward him. A flame struck him, leaving him unconscious. When he awakened, he saw a myriad of colors and three sacred symbols. In the energy and symbols, Usui found his answer. He had become a channel of healing energy to everyone he touched. *Reiki*, the channeling of divine energy through physical touch, was born. Today, thousands of persons, including many Christians such as myself, have learned to channel this divine energy by placing their hands on certain parts of their own or another's body and allowing this divine energy to flow through us to the person in need.

The work of Mikao Usui, along with that of Barbara Brennan and Dolores Krieger, has opened new horizons in the intersection of medicine and religion. In their work, both Brennan, a scientist, and Krieger, a nurse, integrate their strong backgrounds in science and physiology with an awareness of the energy fields that surround and permeate the human body.

With a background in atmospheric physics and spiritual healing, Barbara Brennan's work reflects a creative synthesis of physics, physiology, bioenergetics, and the esoteric realm of auras, chakras, and higher sense perception. While she does not claim to be a conventional Christian, Brennan, like the Worralls and Sanford, believes that everything in the universe is surrounded and connected by energy fields. In the spirit of contemporary physics, Brennan holds that "mass is nothing but a form of energy. Matter is simply slowed down or crystallized energy. Our bodies are energy."[20]

The universe and the human body are composed of various levels of energy. This universal energy field—described by the Chinese as *ch'i*, the Hindus as *prana*, and by the psychiatrist Wilhelm Reich as *orgone*—is the force of creation and growth, the counterforce to entropy, flowing through all things. Although all things are interconnected, each being is surrounded by its own energy fields or auras. These auric fields, now identifiable through Kirlian photography, extend beyond each body and serve as the storehouse for emotions and thoughts that reflect both from and to the body. Brennan believes that these auric fields of energy are the link between biology and psychotherapy.[21] Each auric field is connected with a *chakra*, or energy center, within the body. The *chakras*—the primary ones being associated with areas such as the forehead, throat, heart, solar plexus, etc.—serve as openings for the universal energy to flow in and out of our bodies as they metabolize the energy fields surrounding us.[22] Each *chakra* is also associated with an aspect of human existence—for example, thought, higher spirituality, sexuality, love, physical well-being. When they are open, the *chakras* allow the life-giving energy of the cosmos to flow in and out of one's life and, thus, constantly refresh and replenish oneself.

Illness, in contrast, occurs when the "blocking" of one or more energy centers creates an energy imbalance. All illnesses are "initiated in the energy fields and are then, through time and living habits, transmitted to the body, becoming serious illnesses."[23] When emotional energy is blocked through our reactions to unpleasant situations, this imbalance is reflected both in the aura and in the bodily and psychic functions that mirror that aspect of the human energy field. Imbalance eventually leads to entropy, disease, and death. Since the transformation of energy characterizes the nature of reality, the physical and the psychical can never be separated. Disordered energy in the heart *chakra* relates, for example, to angina and heart disease. Further, Brennan states that "a torn chakra has appeared in every cancer I've seen."[24] At the heart of all illness, Brennan believes, is self-hatred and self-forgetfulness.[25] Accordingly, the experience of illness provides an opportunity to realign oneself with the universal energy and learn those lessons that are pivotal in one's life's journey. Brennan believes that the pain associated with illness may be the catalyst for creative insight. Healing is a spiritual issue. In opening to the universal energy, we align ourselves with the divine presence in the universe, in ourselves, and in higher beings who seek to guide us.

According to Brennan, the task of the healer, or healing companion, is to facilitate the opening and balancing of the energy fields so that the client is restored to dynamic well-being. The process of healing involves the laying on of hands on the body as well as on the subtler energy fields surrounding the physical body. In this process, the healing companion is not merely a channel of energy but a guide whose "high sense perception" (that is, clairvoyant or psychic experience) enables her to see both the causes and cures to illness. Diagnoses and treatment are often intuitively "channeled" from higher spiritual awareness to the healing companion.

Being involved in your own or another's healing is, ultimately, a spiritual vocation. "Becoming a healer means to move toward the universal creative power which we experience as love by reidentifying self with and becoming universal; becoming one with God."[26] Healing is symbiotic: the recipient as well as the healing companion is invited into new worlds of spiritual experience. The unblocking of energy opens us to new emotions and insights and to "higher" powers within ourselves.

In her own work with therapeutic touch, Dolores Krieger, a registered nurse with a doctorate in nursing, has found that the direction of energy is never merely one-dimensional. The simple and easily learned technique of therapeutic touch has been used by nurses in hospitals and emergency rooms as well as by laypersons throughout the United States. In its most basic form, therapeutic touch involves the scanning of a person's body by passing hands slowly over his body and then focusing energy through the hands toward (but not on) the part of the body in most obvious need of care. Although therapeutic touch is essentially nonsectarian and does not directly address spiritual issues, its ultimate goal is to transform the patient from passivity to creativity in the facilitation of her own wellness. According to Krieger:

> The transfer of energy from the person playing the role of healer is usually little more than a booster until the patient's own recuperative system takes over. At best, the healer accelerates the healing process.[27]

From a more explicitly spiritual perspective, Brennan describes this same experience of unblocking emotional energy through the laying on of hands in terms of a spiritual awakening, whose impact brings healing to the whole person.

> The work of a healer is a work of love. The healer reaches into these painful areas of the soul and gently reawakens hope. S/he gently awakens the ancient memory of who the soul is. S/he touches the spark of God in each cell of the body and gently reminds it that it is already God and, already being God, it inexorably flows with the Universal Will towards health and wholeness.[28]

While the tone of pantheism and the interest in clairvoyance characteristic of Brennan's approach may startle and offend some mainline or evangelical Christians, her work, nevertheless, is consistent in practice and intention with the healing ministry of Jesus as it is expressed in the ministry of persons such as Sanford and the Worralls. In a spirit similar to that of Christian healing, Brennan claims that healing is a reflection of the goodness and love at the heart of reality: there is a universal movement toward health and wholeness. Furthermore, Brennan sees the healer as the channel rather than the focus of healing energy. Echoing the ministry of Jesus, Brennan maintains that the basic problems of life are spiritual in nature and that brokenness, or blockedness, of the spirit or body is released through the interplay of the faith and love of the healer and the receptivity and responsibility of the patient.

Yet, in spite of their shared intent with Christian healing, neither Brennan nor Krieger explicitly invokes the name of Jesus as the focal point of their healing work. As they explore methods such as therapeutic touch, Christians are challenged to integrate these practices with the healing power present in Jesus and emerging at the edges of the church today. Just as early Christians adopted and "christianized" the philosophies of Plato and Aristotle to express their understanding of Jesus Christ, today's Christians may utilize *reiki*, therapeutic touch, and the channeling of energy within the context of Christian theology and worship.

The work of Brennan, Krieger, Usui, Sanford, the Worralls, and even Christian Science and New Thought witnesses to the fact that the world of healing and wholeness holds many mysterious and exciting adventures for those who choose to be open to them. We are surrounded by healing energies that open us to experiences far beyond our usual sense perception and quantitative analysis. In contrast to some of these authors, I would identify these experiences not as paranormal but, indeed, as quite normal for persons of faith. Whatever one chooses to call this universal healing energy of God—*chi, prana,* orgone, *reiki,* or the Holy Spirit—we are all surrounded by it and radiate it as we are loving to ourselves and others.

Healing is not a violation of nature, but a manifestation of an everpresent energy residing in the depths of all things. It is my belief that process-relational thought provides a metaphysical vision that not only supports the healing ministries of Sanford, the Worralls, Krieger, Usui, and Brennan but also integrates them with the more orthodox doctrines and practices of mainstream Christianity.

Exploring the Healing Connection

The new enlivening images of the interrelatedness of mind and body, God and the world, the person and her environment, articulated by a process-relational approach, result in new attitudes toward death and dying, health and medicine, and the role of God in human existence. The edges of life and health care are, in fact, pushed outward as they are explored. For those who adhere to mechanistic, substantialist, and closed-system images of reality, there is no room for such novelty and adventure. Mystery, the unknown, is not inviting but fearsome. Authentic "acts of God" can occur only at the beginning or at the end of history. Any other affirmation of God's presence in the ongoing history of the universe is either nonsense, a nuisance, or an unintelligible interruption in the normal workings of natural law. If God acts at all, God can intervene only from the outside of the universe and from the outside of each creature. A world of independent substances, organized in closed systems, not only makes the relation of mind and body a problem, but makes any significant relationship between God and the world an impossibility. The key concept here is relationship. Is God really related to the world and to human life? Does God have any role in the healing of bodies and minds?

The vision of reality articulated in process thought and pioneered in Christian circles by such healers as Agnes Sanford, the Worralls, and Morton Kelsey proclaims that faith, touch, prayer, and spiritual insight do make a difference not only to minds but also to bodies. Furthermore, process-relational thought maintains that God is present within all things, the secular as well as the religious. Indeed, in a world of relationships there can be no strict boundaries between mind and body, religious and secular, client and healing companion, or God and the world.

Today, mainstream and eucharistic churches are breaking the chains of the Newtonian worldview. For more than thirty years Morton Kelsey, an Episcopalian minister and theologian, has provided theoretical and practical guidance for Christians seeking to be part of a healing ministry. At the Washington Cathedral of the Episcopal Church each Thursday morning, worshipers gather for prayer, communion, and the anointing with oil. Recently, even traditionally liberal and rationalistic churches such as the United Church of Christ have formulated services of healing. In its *Book of Worship*, the United Church of Christ, for example, states that "Healing in the Christian sense is the reintegration of body, mind, emotions, and spirit that permits people, in community, to live life fully in a creation honored by prudent and respectful use."[29] The healing power of God's love relates to the totality of human existence and not merely to the human spirit. This dynamic understanding of healing is reflected in the *Book of Worship's* prayer for anointing: "With infinite mercy may God forgive your sins, release you from suffering, and restore you to health and strength."[30]

In the paragraphs that follow, I would like to share my own process-relational theology of healing, which I hope can be affirmed by "modern" Christians. A process theology of healing invites persons to envisage new adventures in the face of the unexpected presence of divine power as well as the unexpected power of faithful persons. The Christian "healers" we have looked at—or, as I prefer, "healing companions," inasmuch as God is the ultimate healer—as well as their non-Christian counterparts, are in surprising agreement as to the nature and prerequisites for the "healing connection." First, they affirm that healing is ultimately an expression of divinity, or universal life energy. This force or energy, whether personal or impersonal, is loving, benevolent, and health-giving in nature. Alignment with the divine energy is the source of health; alienation from this same energy is one of the root causes of illness. As a result of a particular gift or a commitment to disciplined openness, persons like ourselves may become powerful channels of this heal-ing energy and experience extraordinary insights and powers. The experience of this healing energy is not, however, a viola-tion of natural law but is an expression of the deepest and most basic energies of the universe. Apart from Christian Science and other idealist movements in religion, the consensus of healing companions is that healing energy is expressed not merely in the renewing of mind or spirit but also in the restoration of the body. The "healing connection" is ultimately communal or rela-tional in nature insofar as "acts of power" arise from the inter-play of divinity, specific healing companions (including the faithful community), and the one who is healed.

A process-relational perspective also affirms that the ulti-mate source of the healing of body, mind, and spirit is the divine force present in all things. As the previous chapters have suggested, God's presence in the world is best understood as the dynamic and contextual aim toward beauty, complexity, intensity, and wholeness. In contrast to the widely assumed tendency toward entropy characteristic of so-called physical re-ality, God is the source of novelty and evolution as well as order within the physical world. Apart from God, there would be chaos and nothingness. God's ultimate will is toward the ordering and transformation of all that is chaotic, destructive, and alienating in the universe. Put simply, God wills beauty and healing in all things.

The divine will toward beauty and complexity, however, is revealed not merely in moments of religious experience, heal-ing, or reconciliation. The "special acts" of God are a manifesta-tion of God's implicit presence in all things. As I have noted before, the wisdom and power of God are revealed as much in the growing of plants, the normal function of the immune sys-tem, and the digestion of food as they are in moments of reli-gious conversion, mystical experience, or dramatic physi-cal healing. Apart from God's presence in the ordinary and the undramatic, the dramatic and seemingly miraculous could not occur. In spite of our lack of holistic awareness or our tempta-tion to limit God's concern to spirituality alone, the divine en-ergy is present in every element of the universe and in every cell of our bodies. Accordingly, the special acts of power and discernment associated with mysticism and "extraordinary" healings are not the exception but the "norm," as they reflect, albeit in a heightened sense, God's active concern for the universe. From this perspective, the gradual and undramatic healing of a broken limb is as much a revelation of God's presence as a spontaneous and accelerated healing occurring at the prayer service.

Certain moments are more reflective of the divine than others, just as certain moments of our own lives more adequately express our own character and personal values. These are the moments from which religions arise and persons find new and unexpected direction. As process theologian David Griffin points out, "Every event in the world is an act of God in the sense that it originates with an initial aim derived from God. But some will be [God's] acts in a special sense, just as some of a man's external acts are his in a special sense."[31] The divine is creative as well as receptive. Although the "secular" and "religious" manifestations of the divine are equally important in the ongoingness of the universe, those special moments, celebrated by persons and religions as decisive and unique, allow us to glimpse God's deepest intentions for humankind and the universe. As the Gospel of John proclaims, the "light of the world" present in Jesus Christ allows us to encounter the light that shines in all things (John 1:1–9). These heightened moments of God's presence open us to experience God's desire to respond creatively and redemptively to our every need. As the source of all novelty and adventure, God continuously brings forth new possibilities of beauty and wholeness. The presence of God, described in terms of the "word" and "wisdom" of God in Christ, is the source of the evolution of the cosmos and the transformation of human consciousness. It is also the source of the healing of body, mind, and spirit.

In the images of divine salvation within Judaism and Christianity, the presence of God in human and cosmic history is recognized in terms of the interplay of God's spirit of newness and adventure and God's steadfast love and protection. Scripture witnesses to the dynamic, contextual, and creative energy of God. But scripture as well as process-relational theology also recognizes that God's freedom and healing power—that is, God's love—is conditioned by and responsive to the world. Divine power is never absolute; it is always relational. God cannot violate the laws of the universe or the "centeredness" of any person or thing. As the ministry of Jesus attests, where there is great faith or openness, powerful manifestations of the divine occur. Lack of faith can obstruct the healing power of God.

Nevertheless, God's existence makes a difference. Miracles happen even when they are not recognized. Scripture as well as human experience reveals that remarkable acts of healing and liberation occur when we open ourselves to God's ideals for us, both individually and collectively.

As "the best for the impasse," the divine will toward healing and liberation does not reflect an abstract ideal world but the relational real world in which we exist. Accordingly, what appear to be failures in our eyes are, in fact, the deepest manifestations of divine power possible, given the situation. As Whitehead puts it, "Every act leaves the world with a deeper or fainter impress of God. He then passes into his next relation to the world with an enlarged, or diminished, presentation of ideal values."[32]

The emphasis in process-relational thought is that, although God is the ultimate source of healing, God's presence is not the only factor in the healing process. Healing companions often describe themselves as channels or transmitters of divine energy. In fact, we are all "transmitters of divine energy." It is through creaturely affirmation and openness that "special acts" of God occur. The key issue is our willingness to experience God fully and completely in any life situation. Reality is synergistic in nature. I believe that even Jesus' own divinity was neither passive nor predestined, but was the expression of his willingness to experience God fully and completely in each moment of experience. Christ's extraordinary powers reflect his complete alignment with God's presence in his life. Christ's oneness with his divine parent allowed him to reveal, without obstruction, God's will and God's healing power in every encounter. We can strive to do the same.

The unity of divinity and humanity in Christ is paradigmatic of the reality of God within all experience. The "Christ in you" (Colossians 1:27) and "cry of the spirit" in our hearts (Romans 8:26–27) are not objects external to us, but powers residing within us, presenting each person with the possibility of releasing and channeling divinity for herself or others. Accordingly, the principle of "creative transformation" that lies at the basis of healing and religious experience is not restricted to Christ or even to the Christian community. All things reflect God's presence in varying degrees. For those who seek consciously to follow Christ, "to be in Christ is to have the conformation to Christ as the growing center of one's existence."[33]

In becoming attentive to Christ's own energy or "field of force" within us, and to the process of creative transformation that accompanies it, we can share a Christ-like experience. Just as Christ's own faith opened him to levels of power and experience beyond the everyday, we who open ourselves to God through our daily disciplines of "centering " in Christ also experience expanded levels of energy and "higher sense experience," which allow us not only to heal but to have a diagnostic and personal awareness otherwise unavailable to us. For instance, one is able to experience the emotional and spiritual issues related to a particular physical ailment. It is fairly common that an energetic block, perceived through the hands of a healing companion such as a *reiki* practitioner, has a "message" that it releases when touched. The message can be perceived as a word or an image in the mind of the practitioner or the person being treated. In charismatic circles, this awareness in the healing companion is called a "word of knowledge." This information can be helpful in later spiritual or pastoral counseling, or in a simple verbal, confessional exchange and release at the moment of encounter.

Whether this information arises from God, the higher self, or the Holy Spirit, it represents an encounter with a deeper dimension of life. Many persons intuitively perceive such information on a regular basis even without laying on of hands. It is often expected, in fact, among parents with their children. But the dualistic Newtonian-Cartesian worldview has relegated such experiences to the nonsensical world of the "paranormal" and "extrasensory." In fact, intuitive, touch-oriented communication and healing is quite "normal," and a constant potentiality for each of us in a variety of relationships. Such experiences can be understood in the context of the organic nature of reality. Experiences of intuitive wisdom are grounded in the self's openness to its creaturely and divine environment. Such experiences result in a greater sensitivity to the relational nature of life. That is, to open to God and thereby become conformed to the mind of Christ is to experience life, spiritually as well as empirically, from the divine perspective. From such a perspective, divine revelation and healing emerge. We may fully incarnate the highest possibility for the healing of ourselves and others. We can experience both the consciousness and "dynamics" of Christ. In such Christ-like moments, the hidden power of the universe is revealed in a particular moment of time, not as a violation of the laws of nature but as an expression of the divinity immanent within nature. Obviously, such experiences of extraordinary knowledge and power must be conditioned by humility, for all healing and all knowledge are gifts of God's presence in the particular situation. As first-century Corinthians and twentieth-century healing companions have discovered, gifts of revelation or power always imply a finite and relative "receiver." The imperfection of all persons involved in the healing enterprise drives the authentically faithful toward the manifestation of the greatest of all virtues, self-transcendent love.

The manifest power of self-transcending love, as a vehicle of healing, is revealed not only in a life of highly intentional, healing touch but also in a committed life of prayer, meditation, and community involvement. No healing companion operates in a vacuum. Creating or finding a healing community in which to be nurtured as well as to nurture is as vital as daily attention to opening, centering, and grounding oneself in God's healing energy. Praying for others, whether in words or images, heightens the radiation of the energy fields and forms a bridge of united and powerful energy surrounding both the pray-er and the subject of prayer. In a world of relationships, such positive images and feelings of love are not bound by physical proximity but radiate across the universe, surrounding our whole planet with positive energy and light, and providing an opening through which a heightened presence of God may emerge. Such love is both physiological and transpersonal. Such radiations can be "seen" and "measured" by some. Our affirmations, prayers, and images of healing permeate not only our own lives but the psychic and cellular structure of others. In a significant way, our prayers and affirmations become data in the self-creativity and self-realization of others.

Touch and prayer do make a difference and may alter, either gradually or dramatically, one's situation or the life of another—physiologically, psychologically, and spiritually. In this context, a wide variety of symbols of the "healing connection," such as the eucharist, laying on of hands, anointing with oil, and wearing and holding crystals and crosses not only releases the faith of the healing companion and the healee but are also themselves (as a result of the energies that have surrounded their use) "objective" channels through which divine forgiveness, transformation, and healing may be experienced. The transforming power of crystals, for example, depends—like the eucharist—both on the power residing within the object and the purity of heart and love of the practitioner.[34]

In addition to God and the healing companions, the third member of the healing connection is the one for whom healing is asked, that is, the one who consciously or unconsciously seeks healing. Ultimately, there is no distinction between the healing companion and the subject of healing. Both are objects of God's love and care. Both embody in their lives the divine presence. And both, by their openness to that presence, may experience the dramatic or gradual opening of healing energy. To a woman suffering from a chronic illness, Jesus proclaims, "Your faith has made you well." Indeed, our faith creates a lively connection between God, ourselves, and our healing companions. But it is also true that such releases of power may occur without one's knowledge or openness. In such instances, the prayers and images of others contribute to intensifying the field of divine energy surrounding the subject of concern. In so doing, God is enabled to be manifest more fully in that person's life.

In a holographic or relational universe, our thoughts, feelings, and prayers are not private but radiate through all things. Accordingly, the state of our own health or of the world itself is at least partly conditioned by our own personal images of hope or despair. In this context, the new age emphasis on affirmations and creative visualization is a significant contribution to "spiritual technology" in our time. Operating within both conscious and unconscious experience, affirmations orient ourselves toward the positive futures we seek. For example, a Christian might focus regularly on such scriptural affirmations as "nothing can separate me from the love of God," "I can do all things through Christ who strengthens me," or "I am the light of the world." Disciplined use of affirmations transforms one's perception of the world and oneself. This attentiveness to God and the deeper laws of nature creates a spiritual and physical environment in which the divine presence is magnified.

In spite of the occurrence of gradual as well as dramatic healings, one of the greatest arguments against healing is the fact that not everyone is healed. This is especially a problem for those who hold to the traditional doctrine of divine omnipotence. If a person is not healed, then her continuing sickness must be a manifestation of God's will. Another stumbling block in understanding healing arises when healing is viewed as solely contingent on the faith of the healing companion or of the healee. In such a circumstance, the healee may feel himself to be a failure: "If only I had enough faith, I would have been healed." Such experiences of guilt not only block our receptivity to divine energy but may further unleash the forces of entropy and disease within us. Conversely, the linear approach to healing tempts the healing companion, like the contemporary physician, to view himself as the sole cause of the failure or the primary medium of success. In a multidimensional, relational universe, it is impossible to discern merely one cause for illness or healing. Divine activity is limited by creaturely responsiveness. Beyond issues of faith, unfaith, and human freedom, every experience is also influenced by unconscious factors, positive or negative environmental energy, the setting, and the location of a particular moment of our lives within our personal and cosmic context. Indeed, given the interplay of our history and possibilities, not to mention our physical condition, the healing of the spirit rather than the physical body may be the highest possibility. We need to be reminded that although his quest for physical healing remained unsuccessful, the apostle Paul nevertheless received a spiritual healing: "My grace is sufficient for you, for power is made perfect in weakness" (2 Corinthians 12:9).

While the media highlights only spectacular moments of healing and revelation, most healing is gradual, imperceptible, and undramatic even to those within whom it is occurring. But it is tangible and real. Healing results from the interplay of innate recuperative powers, spiritual transformation, and the healing presence of the divine and creaturely communities. Further, in a world in which perpetual perishing and death are inherent in the nature of things, those who define healing solely in terms of physical survival fail to recognize the "many" and the "mini" opportunities for healing the whole person available in each moment of life.

Healing the Dying

In his reflections on his experience following his wife's death, C.S. Lewis suggests ironically that it was Lazarus and not Stephen who was the first martyr of the church, since Lazarus died not once but twice for the faith.[35] Life always ends in death. Even a person fully open to divine energy discovers that her physical energy eventually reaches its limits. For many reasons, most persons who pray for healing experience something far different from the dramatic healings so often celebrated by the media. In his work with children with cancer, Jerry Jampolsky, a psychiatrist and the originator of Attitudinal Healing, sees healing as primarily involving the whole person and not just the body. Health, according to Jampolsky, is ultimately "inner peace."[36] Jampolsky sees healing as the result of a person's removing "the barriers of his perception of love's presence within him."[37] Although physical healing is often celebrated as the primary witness to the uniqueness of Christ, Christ's ability to mediate the experience of grace and forgiveness is, in fact, the basic and most pervasive source of healing. At the heart of the healing connection is the recognition that God is present even at the edges of life. Although dramatic physical healing may be impossible, authentic personal healing of the person may occur at both conscious and unconscious levels.

The spiritual healing companion, like the physician, is called to use her gift to call forth a deeper healing that transcends the healing of the body. Through liturgical laying on of hands, *reiki,* or techniques such as therapeutic touch, we may radiate a sense of comfort, pain relief, and connection with the wider human community. The eucharistic meal may serve to invite us to experience not only death and resurrection but also the gift of forgiveness and "the healing of memories" taught by Dennis and Matthew Linn.[38] By touching a dying person's energy centers and infusing them with divine energy (for example, the heart *chakra* or crown *chakra*), the healing companion may enable the dying person to remain open to the energies of love and spirituality, even as the body is wasting away.

Christianity has always recognized that the death of the person, or the spirit, is always deeper than the death of the body. By our presence, our prayers, and our touch, we as friends and relations may help create a "spaciousness," to use the imagery of Stephen Levine, through which a dying person may awaken to the presence of the divine within. The bridge between life and death is always love, and touch and prayer are the most powerful channels of God's love at the descending edges of life. At the edges of life, the artificial distinctions of life and death, sickness and health, spirituality and secularity, mind and body, are overcome. Even at death there is a healing connection, grounded in the experience that "nothing can separate us from the love of God."

Notes

[1]Edwin Abbot, *Flatland* (New York: Dover Press, 1953), p. 80.

[2]The most notable exception is Morton Kelsey's excellent text *Psychology, Religion and Christian Healing* (New York: Harper and Row, 1988). This is a revision of Kelsey's earlier work *Healing and Christianity.*

[3]Robert Peel, *Health and Medicine in the Christian Science Tradition* (New York: Crossroad, 1988), p. 1.

[4]Mary Baker Eddy, *Science and Health with Key to the Scriptures* (Boston: Trustees Under the Will of Mary Baker Eddy, 1934), p. viii.

[5]*Ibid.*, p. 468.

[6]*Ibid.*, p. 277.

[7]*Ibid.*, p. 153.

[8]*Ibid.*, p. 423f.

[9]*Ibid.*, p. 426.

[10]*Ibid.*, p. 427.

[11]Robert Peel, *Spiritual Healing in a Scientific Age* (San Francisco: Harper and Row, 1987), p. 28.

[12]Mary Baker Eddy, *Science and Health*, p. 146.

[13]*Ibid.*, p. 170.

[14]Agnes Sanford, *The Healing Light* (St. Paul: Macalester Park Publishing, 1972), p. 17.

[15]*Ibid.*, p. 30f.

[16]*Ibid.*, p. 33.

[17]Ambrose and Olga Worrall, *The Gift of Healing* (New York: Harper and Row, 1965), p. 9.

[18]Sanford, *The Healing Light*, p. 72.

[19]*Ibid.*, p. 31.

[20]Barbara Ann Brennan, *Hands of Light* (New York: Pleiades Books, 1987), p. 24.

[21]*Ibid.*, p. 89.

[22]*Ibid.*, p. 45.

[23]*Ibid.*, p. 7.

[24]*Ibid.*, p. 143.

[25]*Ibid.*, pp. 110, 131.

[26]*Ibid.*, p. 28.

[27]Dolores Krieger, *Therapeutic Touch* (Englewood Cliffs: Prentice-Hall, 1979), p. 17.

[28]Brennan, *Hands of Light*, p. 131f.

[29]*United Church of Christ Book of Worship* (New York: United Church of Christ Office for Church Life and Leadership, 1986), p. 306.

[30]*Ibid.*, p. 317.

[31]David Griffin, *A Process Christology* (Philadelphia: Westminster, 1973), p. 215.

[32]Whitehead, *Religion in the Making*, p. 152.

[33]Cobb, *Christ in a Pluralistic Age*, p. 122.

[34]Rose Morningstar, *A Course on Crystals* (New York: Harper and Row, 1989), p. 11.

[35]C.S. Lewis, *A Grief Observed* (New York: Bantam, 1976), p. 47f.

[36]Jerry Jampolsky, *Teach Only Love* (New York: Bantam, 1983), p. 34.

[37]*Ibid.*, p. 40.

[38]Dennis and Matthew Linn, *The Healing of Memories* (Mahweh, N.J: Paulist Press, 1974); *Healing Life's Hurts* (Mahweh, N.J.: Paulist Press, 1978).

6

Death and Spirituality

Death and the Spiritual Quest

A young Indian prince named Gautama lived in blissful innocence, enjoying all the pleasures that life can give, until one day he came upon a corpse. From that moment on, the young prince realized that all things are transitory, that his dancing girls weary and grow old, that kingdoms rise and fall, and that even kings and princes like himself must die. In that moment of dislocation and insight, a spiritual journey began that was to reshape profoundly the Asian world: Gautama would eventually come to be revered as the Buddha, the enlightened one.

Death is a profoundly spiritual issue. Just as the body cannot be separated from the mind, death cannot be separated from the challenges of spiritual growth that occur at every stage of life. In the midst of life, the possibility of death shatters our sense of indestructibility and compels us to go beyond the surface dimensions of life.

Life is a series of deaths and rebirths. Robert Jay Lifton suggests that death anxiety—symbolized by the polarities of connection-separation, movement-stasis, integrity-disintegration—surfaces at each moment of transition in the passage from infancy to old age. As he grieved over his wife's death, C.S. Lewis realized that his bereavement was a chilling reminder to every happily married couple that one of them eventually will be left at the graveside. Yet even when there is death and grief, there is the possibility of new life. As I complete this manuscript, I have fond memories of a wedding I recently performed at the Washington Institute for Attitudinal Healing. The couple had met at a weekend spiritual retreat, following the death of both of their spouses from cancer. Rather than turning their backs on life, they began their healing process by studying the "principles of attitudinal healing," as taught by Jerry Jampolsky and Susan Trout.[1] Their children also became part of this healing process through children's courses at the Institute. At the wedding celebration, there were tears of grief mixed with tears of joy, because both were reminded that their first steps on the healing journey began when each of their deceased spouses sought spiritual care for themselves and their families at the Institute. At the edges of life, when the foundations of our once secure existence are shaking, we seek something within us and beyond us for protection, guidance, and strength, something to enable us to begin again. We seek the spiritual dimension of life.

The quest for a spiritual foundation in a threatening world is portrayed in Madeleine L'Engle's *A Ring of Endless Light*. As she blossoms into womanhood, Vicky Austin finds her safe and sheltered existence shattered by the reality of death. In a world in which death can strike at any moment, Vicky yearns for something stable and secure. Through a friend she becomes acquainted with the dolphins studied by a marine research project, and discovers that she can communicate telepathically with them. Intrigued by the contrast between their carefree, joyful play and her own anxious, sorrow-ridden existence, she asks the dolphins to tell her how they experience the world.

> Dearest Norberta and Njord [the dolphins]. Do you live in the now, or do you project into the future, the way I do, far too often?
>
> I felt a gentle puzzlement coming from Njord....
>
> Norberta?
>
> Again I felt the puzzlement, not puzzlement about her understanding, but my own. Norberta wasn't sure I'd be able to understand.
>
> Try me.

I rolled over onto my back and floated and Norberta moved her great body toward me until we were touching, and I was pressed against the beautiful resiliency of dolphin skin. And a whole series of pictures came flashing across the back of my eyes, in the dream part of my head.

The ocean.

Rain.

A rainbow, glittering with rain.

Snow, falling in great white blossoms to disappear as it touched the sea.

And then the snow turned to stars, stars in the daytime, drenched in sunlight, becoming sunlight.

And the sunlight was the swirling movement of a galaxy and the ocean caught the light and was part of the galaxy and the stars of the galaxies lifted butterfly wings and flew together, dancing.

And then Norberta, with Njord echoing her, began making strange sounds, singing sounds, like the alleluia sounds Basil [another dolphin] had made, and they did something to my understanding of time, so that I saw that it was quite different from the one-way street which was all I knew.[2]

The realities of brokenness and death compel us to seek new and more vital ways of experiencing the world. Whether our search centers around mystical experience, physical healing, or simply coping with the inevitability of death, the quest itself must lead us beyond our ordinary way of experiencing the world. Like the middle-aged Square from *Flatland*, we discover that the world and our own experience are much more surprising and mysterious than we had imagined.

In Western civilization, the wellsprings of the religious and the philosophical adventure find their initial inspiration in the encounter with death. Socrates' death in prison and Jesus' journey to the cross not only inspire two contrasting images of Western spirituality but also proclaim that authentic spirituality requires direct confrontation with one's mortality. Accordingly, Athens, the birthplace of Western philosophy, and Jerusalem, the sacred city of Judaism and Christianity, provide our culture's most fundamental insights into the search for a spirituality of wholeness at the edges of life.

Plato's dialogue, the *Phaedo,* portrays the death of the Athenian philosopher Socrates (469–399 B.C.). On the final day of his life, Socrates' pupils find him quietly awaiting his execution—the penalty he had received for "corrupting" the youth and challenging the religion of the city. As they wait for the appointed time, the grieving disciples express surprise at Socrates' good humor and apparent indifference at his imminent death. In response to their surprise, Socrates replies that, of all persons, the philosopher, the lover of wisdom, should seek death with equanimity, since "all those who betake themselves to philosophy in the right way are engaged in one thing only, namely training themselves for dying and being dead" (64a).[3] According to Socrates, death is the separation of the body and the soul (64c). Since the philosopher's primary concern is to turn from the body to eternal realities of life, death is not to be feared.

From the philosopher's perspective, the lure of the everchanging physical world blinds us to the deeper realities of life. Indeed, in the philosopher's quest for self-awareness, the body is a prison and a hindrance, valuable only insofar as it enables us to pursue the eternal (65a–b). As Socrates puts it, "The philosopher's soul utterly despises his body and flees from it, seeking to be alone by itself" (65d). Only death, the ultimate separation of soul and body, can provide the liberation of the soul, desired by the true philosopher.

Although Plato's later writings present a world-affirming vision of the philosopher's quest, it was Plato's account of his teacher's death in the *Phaedo* that served as the model for the ascetic and world-denying philosophies and practices of gnosticism and the monastic tradition of Christianity. At the heart of this vision is the belief that the soul alone is of value and that the body is either an illusion or, if it is real, a hindrance in the quest for self-awareness. From this perspective, spirituality pertains solely to the life of the spirit. The lover of wisdom yearns for rebirth in a world of eternal perfection and unity, a place where the world of diversity, particularity, and change, the world of bodies, is but a memory.

The Christian tradition sees the death of Jesus as his greatest triumph and the most vivid demonstration of his spiritual commitment and relationship to God. Unlike Socrates, who dies calmly in the company of friends, Jesus dies in abandonment,

humiliation, and agony. Although Jesus anticipates the likeli-
hood of his own death, he faces it with anything but equanimity
and calm. His prayer on the Mount of Olives reveals the spirit of
one who fights against death in all its guises, yet is willing to
accept death as a necessary part of his mission.

> "Father, if you are willing, remove this cup from me; yet,
> not my will but yours be done." Then an angel from heaven
> appeared to him and gave him strength. In his anguish he
> prayed more earnestly, and his sweat became like great
> drops of blood falling down on the ground.
>
> Luke 22:42–44

But even in the darkest hour when he feels forsaken by God,
Jesus does not allow the forces of death to overwhelm his spirit.
His last words are those of affirmation and trust: to the angry
crowds, Jesus says, "Father, forgive them; for they know not
what they are doing" (Luke 23:34). To the dying thief beside
him, he gives acceptance and assurance, "Truly I tell you, today
you will be with me in Paradise" (Luke 23:43). Whereas Socrates'
death is an invitation to contemplate the eternal, Jesus' death is
a call to relationship and forgiveness. For the Christian, the
cross is the deepest revelation of Jesus' spirituality and of the
God he sought to proclaim. The triumph of Easter is, in fact, the
realization of what had already occurred at Calvary—the personal and spiritual transformation of death from alienation into
reconciliation.

For those who affirm the reality of the cross, Jesus' death is
no illusion, but is the revelation of God's concern for the world
in its totality. The physical imagery associated with both the
crucifixion and resurrection proclaim that distinctions between
body and spirit and secular and sacred have no place in the
spiritual life. For those who follow the path of Jesus, God's
redemption occurs in the body as well as in the spirit, in this
world as well as beyond the grave.

The paths of Socrates and Jesus still guide seekers after
truth. Each path offers its own unique vision of the interplay of
mortality and spirituality. In formulating my own theology of
healing and wholeness at the edges of life, I have sought to
honor their spiritual paths. As we reflect on a theology and
spirituality of wholeness and healing, we will explore three of
the most persuasive contemporary options in contemporary
Western spirituality: (1) gnostic images in ancient and new age

philosophies (in particular, *A Course on Miracles*), (2) the "creation spirituality" of Matthew Fox, and (3) a process-relational vision of spirituality. Each of these has been important in shaping my own spirituality by providing insights and spiritual disciplines for my own quest to live fully at the edges of life. The spirituality of healing and wholeness is, as I have suggested throughout this book, a spirituality of life and living. Our vision of God, the world, physical existence, and the purpose of human life is reflected in our own spiritual lives. Since spirituality can never be separated from matters of life, death, and human wholeness, my reflections on spirituality will be grounded in the metaphysical vision and psychological reflections of the earlier chapters. Accordingly, the metaphysical foundations of a process-relational spirituality will be addressed in the briefest manner.

The Gnostic Vision: Ancient and Modern

The spiritual journey always involves an element of restlessness and impatience with the imperfections of ourselves and the world. The process of "centering," essential to spiritual discipline, leads us on an inner journey through which we move from sound to silence, from plurality to unity. In such moments, the lure of the external world is temporarily released as we embark on the search for the divine. Our preoccupation with prestige, wealth, and bodily well-being fades into the background, at least during our times of prayer and meditation.

While our spiritual journey does not require a denying of the world, it requires a transformation of our perception and valuation of the world in which we live. For some seekers this transformation involves the "divinization" of the physical world. Being made holy, the world becomes a sanctuary, reflecting in all its dimensions the presence of God. To other seekers, such as Socrates, the physical world is found to be less friendly. For them, one follows the inner path precisely because the world is a hindrance and prison for the soul that seeks enlightenment.

Although communion with the world is a necessity during our physical lives, it is only a means to a greater end, self-awareness, and is not of value in and of itself. In the West, this latter path, that of world-denial and transcendence, has traditionally been identified with the adventures of gnostics, both ancient and modern. Indeed, gnosticism—from the Greek, "to know"—has in its many faces been the perennial "heterodox" alternative as well as a significant influence upon mainstream, "orthodox" Christian experience.

The gnostic movements of the centuries surrounding the birth of Christ have become especially important in the wake of the Nag Hammadi discoveries and the creative interpretations of gnosticism put forth by Elaine Pagels.[4] Virtually every "new age" or "metaphysical" bookshop displays gnostic writings as if they represented the primary channel of Christian spirituality. These writings were most probably a channel of Christian spirituality, but clearly not a primary one. Gnosticism has distinct ecclesiastical and social dimensions, around which much scholarly debate has occurred. My focus here is not on this debate but on the interplay of metaphysics, death, and spirituality in ancient and contemporary gnostic movements.

In his analysis of the roots of gnosticism, the philosopher Hans Jonas states, "Dread as the soul's response to its being-in-the-world is a recurrent theme in gnostic literature."[5] In the gnostic vision we are aliens, thrown into a hostile world, which does not know us and cannot reveal to us who we really are. We are exiles and strangers in the physical world, in search of salvation and release through our knowledge (*gnosis*) of the ultimate reality lying beyond this world. Whereas mainstream Christian doctrine asserts that the world and physical existence are the good creation of a loving God, gnosticism holds that the world is ultimately a mistake, the creation of inferior gods or, possibly, principles of evil, who have forgotten their own spiritual birthright. According to Jonas,

> the [gnostic] deity is absolutely transmundane, its nature alien to that of the universe, which it neither created nor governs and to which it is the complete antithesis: to the divine realm of light, self-contained and remote, the cosmos is opposed as the realm of darkness.[6]

The world-denial characteristic of Christian gnosticism is reflected in the thought of the early Christian philosopher and heretic Marcion who, according to Elaine Pagels,

> was struck by what he saw as the contrast between the creator-God of the Old Testament, who demands justice and punishes every violation of his law, and the Father whom Jesus proclaimed—the New Testament God of forgiveness and love. Why, he asked, would a God who is

"almighty"—all-powerful—create a world that includes suffering, pain, disease—even mosquitoes and scorpions? Marcion concluded that these must be two different Gods.[7]

Accordingly, whether they affirmed a dualism of spirit and matter due to our spiritual ignorance or to the conflict of opposing spiritual forces within the universe, the gnostics of the first few centuries of the Christian era "exorcised" the divine presence from the physical universe. As the writer of the recently discovered gnostic Gospel of Thomas proclaims, "if spirit came into being because of the body, it is a wonder of wonders. Indeed, I am amazed that this great wealth [the spirit] has made its home in this poverty [the body]."[8] Although the body is real, it is of no value and is, as Socrates had perceived, a hindrance in the spiritual quest. Liberation and salvation, accordingly, cannot be found in the mundane and changing world.[9]

Even the death of Christ, so essential to the orthodox tradition, is seen as an illusion from the gnostic perspective. Although Jesus' body suffered, Jesus' divinity was beyond joy or sorrow. In the gnostic *Acts of John*, Jesus is seen not as a human being at all, but as a spiritual being who adapted himself to human perception.[10] The death of Jesus or of any person is ultimately an illusion—and quite possibly a blessing, enabling the soul to have further adventures apart from its bodily prison. In the spirit of Socrates, gnosticism sees the spiritual adventurer as an alien, whose search for an eternal homeland is a constant preparation for death.

Although the gnostic movements of the first few centuries after Christ have disappeared, the gnostic spirit has never died. The gnostic image of spiritual homelessness, asceticism, world-denial, and divine transcendence has surfaced, in various forms and with various emphases, in mainstream Christendom as well as in contemporary new age movements.

The metaphysics and spirituality surrounding *A Course on Miracles* provides one of the most interesting and insightful "new age" and contemporary gnostic alternatives to mainstream Christianity. The *Course*, as it is called, claims to be a divinely channeled revelation of Christ to humans of our time. From 1965 to 1972 Helen Schucman, a research psychologist and self-professed "militant atheist," received dictation from an "inner voice" that called itself the Christ. While Schucman never became a member of any organized religion, the "dictations" of the *Course* responded to her own quest to find peace in a world of conflict. Since that time, the three volumes that make up *A Course on Miracles* have come into the hands of countless seekers of truth and vital spiritual experience.[11]

The *Course* contains not only philosophical ruminations but also daily studies and affirmations, similar to the *Daily Word* or *Upper Room*, that enable the student to integrate its challenging metaphysical system with her daily life. Although no organized religious body has formed around the *Course*, its followers study privately, gather in local study groups, and often participate in Unity or Religious Science churches. A few of its adherents from mainline churches read the *Course* as a companion to their Bibles. I have spent a number of years studying the *Course*, initially as a form of daily spiritual discipline and insight during a difficult period in my life, later as a scholar seeking to integrate and critique the *Course* from a Christian perspective.

As a book of spiritual guidance, the *Course* claims to be a contemporary revelation of Christ whose purpose is to purify traditional Christianity by correcting its false understanding of God, the world, sin, and the human self.[12] The aim of the Course is to remove:

> the blocks to the awareness of love's presence, which is your natural inheritance....The Course can therefore be summed up very simply in this way: Nothing real can be threatened. Nothing unreal exists....Herein lies the peace of God.[13]

The key issue for human life then is the correct awareness of reality. True knowledge and reality relate to what is always one and changeless. "Whatever is true is eternal, and cannot change or be changed. Spirit is therefore unalterable because it is absolutely perfect."[14] In contrast to the unity of which the *Course* speaks, our ordinary experience of the world is characterized by change and separation, physical existence, fear, isolation, and defensiveness. Indeed, all these everyday realities are a result of our ignorance of the unity of life.

Whereas the early gnostics saw the world of change as real but evil, the *Course*, not unlike Christian Science, sees the physical world as an illusion, created by our projection of sin, guilt, and separation. As one commentator points out, the *Course* holds that "the world is an illusion. It does not actually exist. It is a dream, and we are the ones, billions of years ago, who fell asleep and dreamed it up. Heaven is the only reality."[15] In language reminiscent of gnosticism, the *Course* maintains that the world projected by our sense of separation was made as an attack on God.[16]

The *Course* is grounded in a nondualistic, or monistic, metaphysical vision, which maintains that Unity or God alone exists. In contrast to traditional Jewish and Christian cosmology, the *Course* holds that the world was not created by God, since there is no point of contact between eternity and time. "God only created the changeless."[17] Thus, according to the *Course*, Christianity rests on the misconception that the world is sacred since God created it.[18] "God did not make the body, because it is destructible, and therefore not part of the Kingdom. The body is a symbol of what you think you are. It is clearly a separation device, and therefore does not exist."[19] From the perspective of the *Course*, the Word cannot be made flesh nor can God be present in the physical universe, since ultimately there is no translation between different orders of reality—spirit and matter, reality and illusion. The world of bodies and separate things is a projection of the mind, possessing no reality of its own.

According to *A Course on Miracles*, the ultimate problem in human life is the perception of separation. Whereas in reality each being is a part of God, an idea in the Divine Mind, our attachment to separation, guilt, and judgment creates the world of anxiety, pain, and opposition that we experience. Salvation is the healing of perception by which we awaken from the dream of separation into the reality of eternal and unchanging spirit. When we awaken from the dream, we discover that sin, death, illness, and separateness are all equally unreal. Spirit alone exists.

As children of God, we are essentially one with each other. Separation is not a fact but a perception. Yet, in the language of poetry, the *Course* suggests that God cannot fully be complete until each child becomes aware of her or his true spiritual nature. "As long as a single 'slave' remains to walk the earth, your release is not complete. Complete restoration of the Sonship is the only goal of the miracle-minded."[20] In words that echo traditional understandings of the grace of God, the *Course* maintains that we are already saved and united with God; we are merely unaware of it.

The *Course*, despite its apparent similarity with traditional Christian thought, proclaims that "atonement in physical terms is impossible."[21] Like its gnostic predecessors, the *Course* sees the cross of Christ solely in spiritual terms. It is nonsense to speak of a crucifixion or resurrection in physical terms. The journey toward oneness is adventure of the spirit, which nurtures greater and greater detachment from physical existence. Accordingly, issues of health and justice are peripheral in the spiritual journey. Illness, for example, is a result of the perception of separation; it has no actuality. Although medicine, laying on of hands, and crystals have no inherent value, they may be used as "compromises," or convenient illusions, which activate a temporary and intermediate healing belief.[22]

In the spirituality of the *Course,* issues of social justice and human liberation are equally illusory. Consistent with its metaphysical idealism, the *Course* counsels that one should "seek not to change the world, but choose to change your mind."[23] Kenneth Wapnick holds that our "function in the world is not to feed the hungry, free the oppressed, or serve any other social cause. How can we serve a world that is not there?"[24] Accordingly, the *Course* is silent on issues of peace and justice as they relate to the world of bodies. In all encounters, the goal is to awaken from the dream of separation and realize our spiritual nature by letting go of all that alienates us from our true selves and our brothers and sisters in Christ. From the *Course's* perspective, the only form of human liberation is grounded in the inner experience of forgiveness and spiritual unity.

The power of the *Course* is found in its unrelenting message of unity and forgiveness. Despite our feelings of lostness and alienation, once we penetrate the illusions of matter we will discover that we are one with God. It maintains that we are never alone, for the Holy Spirit answers every call for help. Eventually all of God's children will find themselves. Salvation is grounded in a transformed perception of the world through which one moves from separation to oneness.

I find that the *Course* is correct in its perception that the world of separate, unrelated substances is an illusion and a source of unhappiness. In agreement with the *Course,* process-relational thought maintains that the mechanistic and dualistic worldview is, indeed, the primary illusion from which we need to be liberated. The *Course* and process-relational thought both maintain that a change in our perception of the world implies a new way of response to it.

However, even though the *Course* shares a common language with traditional Christian thought, its worldview is vastly different. Christians are challenged to reflect upon whether the *Course*'s denial of God's relationship to the physical world negates its use as a tool for Christian spiritual discipline. At issue is a basic question of doctrine and practice: can mainline Christians learn from people who deny the traditional Christian worldview? Although I would answer in the affirmative, I believe that Christian appropriation of nontraditional spiritual disciplines and worldviews, including the affirmations of the *Course*, must be grounded in the critical affirmation of God's presence in the world and the goodness of physical existence. If they are to use the *Course* creatively, Christians must read its pages in conjunction with their study of the world-affirming spirituality of the Bible.

I believe that the *Course*'s denial of the physical world weakens its value for a holistic spirituality. In its emphasis on the unreality of the physical world, the *Course* undermines its own image of divine love. Although the language of the *Course* often suggests that God cares for the world, the metaphysics of the *Course*, like those of classical Christianity, renders any authentic relationship between God and God's children questionable. While the god envisaged in the *Course* may love the spirit, this god can neither empathize with nor experience the pain and brokenness we feel at the edges of life. God experiences only the unity and the bliss of connectedness. The pain of the dying and the grieving is alien to this impersonal and unfeeling deity.

The central issue of a spirituality of health and wholeness is God's relation to the world and human existence. The *Course* is unequivocal in its contradiction of traditional and process-relational Christianity: God did not create the physical world. Although the *Course* speaks of many paths to the divine, it also maintains that there can be no compromise of its nondualistic idealism. In an argument echoing the logic of biblical fundamentalists, the *Course* cautions that it "will be believed in its entirety or not at all. For it is wholly true or wholly false, and cannot be partly believed. And you will either escape from misery or not at all."[25] If this is truly the case, world-affirming Christians would be forced to abandon the *Course* in the same manner as many contemporary persons were driven from Christianity by the "either-or" approach of fundamentalism.

In contrast to the *Course*, process-relational metaphysics embraces the totality of our experience as essential to the spiritual journey. Although the *Course*'s description of death as an illusion deprives death of its ultimacy, its belief that death and bodily existence are illusions may encourage feelings of guilt and inadequacy among those who experience prolonged physical and mental suffering. Furthermore, if God is immune from the pain of the world, then in spite of its emphasis on healing, the god of the *Course* provides little comfort to the dying and the grieving.

Its value as an aid to spiritual growth notwithstanding, the *Course*, like its gnostic predecessors, confuses issues of value with issues of metaphysics. The "superiority" of the spirit to the flesh in the spiritual quest, and the need to remove oneself from the distractions of daily life in order to tap the depths of the soul, do not necessarily imply, as the *Course* maintains, that the world is an illusion. From a process-relational perspective, the experience of connectedness is basic to reality. As the healing ministry of Jesus proclaims, issues of embodiment and spirituality are essential to God's own quest for unity and wholeness. Caring for others means caring for their bodies and their political well-being as well as their souls. In contrast to the disembodied spirituality of the *Course*, process spirituality encourages spiritual adventurers to discern the presence of God at every level of reality, even within the experiences of separation and brokenness.

Creation Spirituality: ### Matthew Fox and the Celebration of Embodiment

One of the most creative and controversial theologians in recent years is the Roman Catholic priest Matthew Fox. As the director of the Institute for Creation Spirituality in northern California, Fox seeks to integrate theological reflection with practical spirituality. Fox contends that Christian faith needs to reclaim a creation-oriented vision of reality to serve as the foundation of its spirituality. For centuries, mainstream Christianity has been dominated by the "fall-redemption" model, which sees sin as the primary metaphor through which we can understand human existence and our relationship to God. Although Fox does not deny the reality of sin, he contends that the world is best understood in terms of the goodness and beauty of creation and human life. Before we are sinners we are, first of all, God's beloved and beautiful children. In theological language, grace is prior to sin. Fox suggests that Christianity's emphasis on sin and redemption as the primary model for the God-world relationship has led to the destructive dualisms that plague the modern world: humankind and nature, spirit and flesh, masculine and feminine, spirituality and justice.

According to Fox, the revival of creation-centered spirituality is not a luxury; it is a necessity. Indeed, the marriage of the fall-redemption model with the Cartesian-Newtonian image of reality has left in its wake not only intellectual polarization but ecological destruction, unstable international relations, the abandonment of the dying and the unproductive, and the complacent acceptance of massive starvation. Instead of focusing on sin, Fox maintains that Christianity must emphasize the essential goodness of embodiment, sexuality, and nature. Whereas the fall-redemption paradigm devaluates bodily existence as a vehicle for sin, creation spirituality embraces the body as an essential component in spiritual growth. Whereas fall-redemption theology looks beyond this world for eternal life, creation theology seeks the presence of God in this world. Whereas fall-redemption theology affirms the transcendence and otherness of God, creation theology is grounded in the reality of the "cosmic Christ," within whom "we live, move, and have our being." In the spirit of process-relational thought, Fox affirms a "panentheistic" vision of God. This "panentheistic" vision of God's relationship to the world is the ultimate foundation for creation spirituality.

> Panentheism...means "God is in everything and everything is in God." This experience of the presence of God in our depth and of Dabhar [the creative energy or word of God] in all the blessings and sufferings of life is a mystical understanding of God....Panentheism is a way of seeing the world sacramentally. Indeed, as we have seen previously, in the creation-centered tradition, the primary sacrament is creation itself—which includes every person and being who lives.[26]

In contrast to the image of divine clockmaker, characteristic of the Cartesian-Newtonian paradigm, creation theology affirms that God is related to the world in such a way that all of life is holy and all things contribute to the divine experience. In a dynamic, pulsating, and constantly birthing universe, we are called to be co-creators with God by using the materials of our lives in the creation of our own unique work of art, our own lives.[27] Although spirituality, for Fox, still involves times for centering and quiet, the contemplative path leads to an active life of creativity, celebration, playfulness, and embodiment. Every relationship and every aspect of our lives (spirit, body, sexuality) is the material from which a spirituality of creation emerges. In contrast to the dualism fostered by sin-oriented theologies, creation spirituality holds that all things are ultimately related and interconnected. "We live in an illusion of separateness and ego-differentiation, but in reality we are already united, already part of one another, especially where our depths and recesses lie."[28]

In a sacramental universe, even death has a role in the spiritual journey. Whereas the gnostic perspective sees death as an illusion and fall-redemption theologies see death primarily in terms of sin and eternal life, creation theology sees death as part of the natural cycles of life. Dying, like birthing and playing, is sacramental.

The creation-centered spiritual tradition does not teach fear about death. In fact, the trust one learns about love, life, and ecstasy and the pain that accompanies every layer of ecstatic living carry through in the death experience as well. Death too can be trusted. And in a real sense we are entrusted with death so that we ought to be reverencing that aspect of living as much as any other aspect....The very awesomeness of death experiences unveils for us—and for some people for the very first time— the cosmic depth of our lives, the cosmic connections of our lives.[29]

Fox claims that "we must embrace our pain as pain and use it as fuel for our journey."[30]

Creation-centered spirituality, as articulated by Matthew Fox, gives us the broad outlines of a process-relational spirituality of healing and wholeness at the edges of life. In the following section, I will further articulate a theology of healing and wholeness building on the insights of process-relational theology, creation spirituality, and *A Course on Miracles.*

A Spirituality of Wholeness at the Edges of Life

Spirituality and metaphysics are intimately related. The classical and gnostic visions of spirituality are grounded in a hierarchical vision of reality that exalts being over becoming, independence over relatedness, and spirit over matter. Accordingly, Western spirituality has defined God primarily in terms of change-lessness, transcendence, and omnipotence. Our world of change, of birthing and dying, of sin and reconciliation, of loving and learning, was seen merely as a preparation or testing ground for eternal life. In light of the changeless perfection of God and heaven, it was easy to affirm that "this world is not my home, I'm just a-passing through." Although the finality of death played a significant role both in popular religion and in monastic life, the confrontation with pain and death was often neglected. When suffering and death have been acknowledged as aspects of the spiritual journey, they have typically been understood as "tests" sent by an omnipotent god to strengthen and purify the believer's faith or as the prelude to divine judgment. Although the cross is at the heart of Christian spirituality, rarely has the cross been employed as the metaphor by which to understand God's na-ture and presence in the "many" and "mini" deaths we experi-ence. Death and brokenness have seldom been affirmed as windows through which we might experience God's loving pres-ence in our lives.

In chapter three, I suggested that the dying-rising God is the ultimate inspiration for a lively death. Accordingly, our vi-sion of God shapes our understanding of spirituality at the edges of life. In contrast to the traditional images of God, process-relational thought describes God in terms of relatedness, be-coming, suffering, and adventuring. Divine perfection is found in the dynamic interplay of being and becoming within the divine nature and the God-world relationship. The world of perpetual perishing is as dear to God as the world of eternity.

A process-relational spirituality of death and dying rests on the reinterpretation of God's knowledge, presence, and power. Traditional Christian theology has understood divine power ei-ther in terms of the eternal and unalterable will of God or the special saving acts of God. This understanding of God has im-plied, on the one hand, that God is responsible for the evil and pain of the world and, on the other, that God is revealed only within the narrowly religious sphere of life. In contrast to this view, process-relational thought maintains that all things reflect the presence of God. As Whitehead put it, "Every act leaves the world with a deeper or fainter impress of God."[31]

In contrast to those who confine God's presence in the uni-verse solely to the moral and spiritual life, I affirm that divine omnipresence implies that God is revealed in everything, including the natural world and the workings of our bodies. The presence of God is typically identified with moments of self-transcendence, worship, and moral decision-making. However, God is equally and perhaps more foundationally present in drops of experience involving natural laws: minerals, vegetation, blood cells, and amoeba. Creation is a revelation of God's presence. All things, accordingly, are icons, or windows, revealing the divine. All experiences, including pain, anxiety, and the dying process, are revelations of God's presence to those who have eyes to see. Process spirituality is rooted in the affirmation that God can be directly encountered in all things and not merely in the narrowly religious sphere of life. From a process-relational perspective, spiritual discipline is the process of discerning and bringing to conscious awareness the presence of God in all things. With Meister Eckhart, I affirm that "all creatures are words of God" for those who have awakened to God's presence.[32]

Process spirituality nurtures a spirituality of becoming. God's presence is profoundly fluid and changing, dynamic and contextual, in its expression. God's presence in the world is not confined to any form or model. God may appear under virtually any guise, even "the least of these." As that which lures us toward novelty and adventure, God's response to human need is surprising and unexpected. Whereas traditional doctrines of divine power and presence encouraged passivity before the will of God, the "persuasiveness" characteristic of the process-relational vision of God encourages adventure, novelty, and surprise. The "will of God" seeks surprise and adventure just as much as obedience. Authentic spirituality is synonymous with personal creativity.

Process thought proclaims the vision of a passionate, empathetic, and adventurous God. Divine love is revealed in God's embrace of everything. In the divine experience, nothing is lost. God experiences the pain, the brokenness, the sin, and even our illusions about the world. But God is not a victim of the world's pain. Even the "wreckage" of the universe—the results of illusion, conflict, and separation—is welcomed into the divine experience. God constantly transforms the divine experience of the world so that beauty and redemption might burst forth from the brokenness of life. A God of process and becoming embraces and integrates light and darkness, birth and death, pain and pleasure.

If the core of spiritual life involves our imitation or participation in the divine life, then a spirituality of healing and wholeness at the edges of life finds its primary inspiration in the very becoming and transformation characteristic of the divine experience itself. Imitation of God leads us not to abandon the world of flesh and ambiguity but to embrace and perceive the world from a wider perspective. Spirituality, as both the *Course on Miracles* and Matthew Fox proclaim, is a matter of perception. To those who have awakened to the presence of God in all times and places, every experience is a revelation, all ground is holy. Since the world lives by its incarnation of God, even our encounter with pain and death reveals God. Those who embrace the totality of life as a revelation of God discover wholeness and reconciliation where life seems most hopeless and precarious, for even in hopelessness and agony God is present, sharing our pain and guiding us toward the highest possibility available to us. The recognition of the divine presence even in the "dark" moments of life inspires the sense of gratitude, expressed poetically by St. Francis of Assisi.

> And thou, most kind and gentle death,
> waiting to hush our latest breath,
> Alleluia! Alleluia!
> Thou leadest home the child of God,
> And Christ our Lord the way hath trod,
> O praise ye! O praise ye!
> Alleluia! Alleluia! Alleluia![33]

Our spiritual journey is not a process of self-mortification or world-denial. It is a quest for beauty of experience. Whereas beauty and pain are often seen as antithetical, process-relational spirituality maintains that our moments of pain and helplessness bear within them the seeds of intensity, beauty, and richness of experience. To experience the one God in the "many" and "mini" deaths is to make the whole of our lives a dialogue with the divine. In experiencing God's presence in all things—in the joyful and in the sorrowful, in the mystical and in the mundane—we are inspired to have a sense of trust in the universe, in one's present experience, and in the God whose love permeates even the darkest and most painful moments of life. As the psalmist proclaims,

> If I say, "Surely the darkness shall cover me,
> and the light around me become night,"

even the darkness is not dark to you;
for night is as bright as the day,
for darkness is as light to you.
                    Psalm 139:11–12

In our acknowledging and experiencing the grief over a lost child, a lost childhood, a lost job, or a lost future, a new sense of sympathy, acceptance, and centeredness—indeed, a new self— may be born.

As the spirit of life, God embraces all things and guides all persons and things toward wholeness and beauty. Within the universe and within this divine experience, there are no fixed boundaries. Indeed, God's divinity is found precisely in the fact that God excludes nothing from the process of redemption. God's tender care that nothing be lost, not even the sparrow or the hair of our heads, embraces and transforms all things—physical, spiritual, joyful and painful. Those who follow God are invited to seek a similar inclusiveness by embracing, transforming, and divinizing the totality of their own experience. In so doing, the adventurer experiences the "real presence" of Christ in its many forms. Hospitable to all things, we as seekers can rediscover the sense of unity and connectedness that is at the heart of life itself even at its edges. The sense of separation, described by *A Course on Miracles* as the root of alienation and ignorance, is then transcended.

Yet, in contrast to *A Course on Miracles*, a process-relational spirituality maintains that the body is not a hindrance to the experience of connectedness. Our problem lies not in our physical existence itself but in our misperception and blindness to the interdependence of the ourselves and the world. As a reflection of divinity, our bodies may inspire and connect as well as blind and separate. For those who have experienced the connectedness of life, the focus is shifted from *my* pain or *my* joy to *the* pain and *the* joy that flow through God and all things, including our bodies. We must always remember that God's love of the world and our bodies is incarnational. It was revealed in Jesus of Nazareth, the newborn babe and the dying savior, and it is revealed in our own births and deaths. As we open to our deepest self, the "Christ within," we experience the rhythm of life that touches all things. Nothing is alien: the self, like the divinity it imitates, radiates to include all things. As we embrace equally the "opposites of life," we hold experiences such as anxiety, agony, inconvenience, and chemotherapy in creative contrast with experiences of sunsets, ecstasy, laughing children, snowflakes, and chanting monks.

The path to beauty of experience varies from person to person and from time to time. Nothing is excluded from our spiritual growth. The conventional as well as the novel may equally contribute to spiritual growth. For me, as a Christian, my spirit has been nurtured by participating regularly in practices as diverse as chanting, psychotherapy, meditation, Ignatian Bible study, *reiki*, laying on of hands, attitudinal healing, and psychosynthesis.

Our highest self or "the Christ within" is not a static deposit, but a many-faceted and everflowing stream of inspiration within ourselves. I have never experienced a life-threatening illness, but I have experienced the deathful life of alienation from my body and my emotions. It took me nearly half a lifetime to discover that emotional expression and embodied existence are neither prisons nor hindrances to my own spiritual growth. I have come to experience embodiment and the whole range of emotional experience as revelations of God and adventures in self-discovery.

Nevertheless, I say this while fully realizing that embodiment is a particular problem for the dying. The body, once a friend, is now an enemy whose pain may potentially deaden the higher spiritual faculties. At the edges of life, the body may seem anything but a "temple" or "embodiment" of the spirit of God. At such moments, acquaintances have told me that they wished the body were an illusion from which they could be delivered, or that body and spirit could be separated as easily as dualism maintains. Yet, over and over again, "pioneering explorers" at the edges of life tell us that even physical pain can be experienced as a vehicle for self-transformation. In opening to the interrelatedness of life and the totality of one's experience, pain is relativized and becomes but one aspect of experience. In embracing pain, we participate in the divine suffering and transformation moving through all things. Our suffering becomes the suffering of God, and God's transformation becomes our own transformation. All that we experience is also God's experience, and God's experience radiates back to us, if we are attuned to it. We become co-creators with God in the redemption of a suffering world (Romans 8:18–23).

Without diminishing the agony of body and spirit, even the pain of cancer or AIDS may be experienced as a window through which self-acceptance, love, and divine companionship may be revealed. The process of taking chemotherapy or receiving medication becomes a sacrament through which we share in the body of Christ and the light of the world. We may, as Native American wisdom proclaimed, "take our medicine in a sacred way."

We all encounter life's edges at various times in our lives. For these edges to become "growing edges," be they at the edge of life called death or merely at an edge called midlife transition, opening to God involves the simplest, yet most profound, acceptance of the reality of the present moment as a means of God's self-revelation within our souls. In such moments, the voice of our highest self—the Christ within the depths of self-creation—is found. As we let go of outworn habits and roles, of expectations and interpretations, the presence of God in the self may be felt for the first time in one's life. We discover, with the apostle Paul, that beneath all of our triumphs and all our fears is our ultimate unity with God: "I have been crucified with Christ; and it is no longer I who live, but it is Christ who lives in me" (Galatians 2:20). In its very ambiguity, life once more becomes surprising and graceful. Yet this wholehearted acceptance and openness to life is a profound act of trust. As we explore the edges of our experience, we find courage in the discovery that our pain is not the only reality and that as we "descend into hell," there is light, for even the farthest and darkest edges of life are filled with the presence of God.

Notes

[1]Jerry Jampolsky, *Love Is Letting Go of Fear* (Milbrae, CA: Celestial Arts, 1979); *Teach Only Love* (New York: Bantam, 1983); *Good-bye to Guilt* (New York: Bantam, 1985). Susan Trout, *To See Differently* (Washington, D.C.: Three Roses Press, 1990).

[2]Madeleine L'Engle, *A Ring of Endless Light* (New York: Dell, 1981), p. 276f.

[3]R. Hackforth, translator and commentator, *Plato's Phaedo* (Cambridge: Cambridge University Press, 1971). Citations from the *Phaedo* follow each quotation.

[4]Elaine Pagels, *The Gnostic Gospels* (New York: Random House, 1979).

[5]Hans Jonas, *The Gnostic Religion* (Boston: Beacon Press, 1967), p. 229.

[6]*Ibid.*, p. 42.

[7]Elaine Pagels, *The Gnostic Gospels*, p. 33.

[8]*Ibid.*, p. 32.

⁹*Ibid.*, p. 174.

¹⁰*Ibid.*, p. 87.

¹¹*A Course on Miracles* consists of three volumes: the text, which presents the metaphysical and psychological foundations for the *Course*; the workbook, which has daily exercises and affirmations that embody in a practical sense the teachings of the *Course*; and a manual for the teacher, which proclaims that each student is also a teacher in the path of self-awareness.

¹²Robert Perry, *An Introduction to the Course on Miracles* (Fullerton: Miracle Distribution Center, 1989), p. 4.

¹³*A Course on Miracles: Text* (Tiburon, California: Foundation for Inner Peace, 1975), Introduction.

¹⁴*Ibid.*, p. 10.

¹⁵Perry, *Introduction to the Course on Miracles*, p. 19.

¹⁶*A Course on Miracles: Workbook* (Tiburon, California: Foundation for Inner Peace, 1975), p. 403.

¹⁷*A Course on Miracles: Text*, p. 95.

¹⁸Kenneth Wapnick, *Love Does Not Condemn* (Roscoe: New York: Foundation for "A Course on Miracles," 1989), p. 6.

¹⁹*Ibid.*, p. 97.

²⁰*Ibid.*, p. 13.

²¹*Ibid.*, p. 18.

²²*Ibid.*, p. 20.

²³*Ibid.*, p. 415.

²⁴*Ibid.*, p. 511.

²⁵*A Course on Miracles: Text*, p. 440.

²⁶Matthew Fox, *Original Blessing* (Santa Fe, New Mexico: Bear and Company, 1983), p. 90.

²⁷*Ibid.*, p. 217.

²⁸*Ibid.*, p. 280.

²⁹*Ibid.*, p. 86.

³⁰*Ibid.*, p. 142.

³¹Whitehead, *Religion in the Making*, p. 152.

³²Matthew Fox, editor and commentator, *Breakthrough: Meister Eckhart's Creation Spirituality in New Translation* (Garden City, New York: Image Books, 1980), p. 58.

³³St. Francis of Assisi, "All Creatures of Our God and King."

7

Epilogue: Adventure and Immortality

The Hope of Immortality

In 1980 my family and I lived in Tucson, Arizona. Not far from our home was a Christian commune, whose members lived in constant expectation of the second coming of Christ. That year, it became clear to them that the end was near and soon the earth would be destroyed. Members of the group sold their homes, quit their jobs, and migrated from the desert plains to the Catalina Mountains overlooking Tucson, in hope that as the flatlands and their inhabitants were scorched they would be rescued by the coming Christ.

In the face of death and destruction, we are always tempted to isolate ourselves from the rest of humanity. Ironically, our traditional Christian vision of survival after death, initially intended to be a comfort, consolation, and invitation to adventure for humankind, has itself been a source of personal and spiritual alienation and anxiety. The expectation of survival after death has been accused of being an impediment to achieving justice and human well-being during the present life. The fear of endless torture beyond the grave has led some to see faith in God as a sound business transaction, while others have lived in terror

159

because they could not believe the dogmas of Christianity. Despite the ambiguity surrounding survival after death, the hope for survival has for the most part played a positive role in the human adventure. In the face of death, the hope that the human spirit is not confined to the brief years of bodily existence has inspired courage, self-sacrifice, and adventure.

I have found that many contemporary Christians are ambivalent about survival after death. "Old line" liberal Christians have maintained that the hope for personal survival after death is peripheral to Christian faith. References to the traditional notions of heaven, hell, and purgatory are absent from many contemporary theological writings and almost nonexistent in the liberal pulpit. At its best, liberal Christianity has sought to maintain a certain agnosticism about matters which can neither be verified nor falsified "scientifically." At its worst, liberalism has allowed philosophical and scientific empiricism to determine the boundaries of human hope. In so doing, the liberal tradition has abandoned the sense of mystery and adventure necessary to vital religious experience, confining the human spirit to the prison of the present moment.

This reaction is in part related to the rejection of the conservative dualism of heaven and hell. Sharp distinctions between the saved and the unsaved—especially when these dichotomies disregard the relativities of culture, environment, and religious commitment—seem morally repugnant. Further, when the hope for an afterlife becomes a justification for inequities in this life, humanists as well as Christians logically assume that the doctrine of survival after death must be discarded as both morally and socially harmful. The conservative dichotomy of the saved and the unsaved encourages persons to be complacent not only about the fate of other persons but also about the fate of the earth. Liberalism has rightly discerned that hope for the future cannot be asserted at the expense of the needs of the present. Hope for the future, if it is to be meaningful, must not be restricted to the favored few, whether they be orthodox believers or members of the human species. The hope for healing and wholeness must be planetary as well as personal.

Process philosopher Charles Hartshorne, in particular, has challenged the idea of personal immortality. According to Hartshorne, the only theologically defensible doctrine of immortality is "objective immortality." This immortality involves the contribution our lives make to God's experience. While we perish subjectively, our lives become part of God's own experience. Hartshorne maintains that authentic immortality is not to be found in the self-interested notion of individual subjective immortality. Our commitment to service and self-actualization is not merely for ourselves; it enriches everlastingly the divine experience. In so doing, our lives become acts of worship and sacrifice to the one immortal God. Hartshorne believes that traditional doctrines of subjective immortality make God a means to personal happiness rather than the focus of all our efforts, the ultimate object of worship. Those who maintain that belief in God is meaningless apart from the affirmation of our personal immortality have forgotten that the chief end of human life is to "glorify God." Any vision of personal survival must have God, rather than our own personal happiness, as its primary focus.

Psychologists and new age visionaries suggest that persons and institutions flourish by affirmation rather than negation. From this perspective, the uncritical liberal and secular negations of survival after death blind their adherents to the possibilities of novel and changing visions of the afterlife and resources for imagination and self-realization in this life. They forget that the chief end of humankind is not only to "glorify God" but also to "enjoy God forever." The hunger for an image of survival after death is evident in the proliferation of movies such as *Flatliners*, *Ghost*, and *Beetlejuice*. Today, our hopes for survival after death are fed more by Hollywood screenwriters than by ministers and theologians. In the religious community, only fundamentalists, evangelicals, and "new agers" seem to speak with any confidence about the afterlife.

In contrast to liberal Christianity's agnosticism, Christian fundamentalism exudes not only a certainty about survival after death but also an apparent "gift" of insight into the identities of those who will be saved and those who will not. What liberalism has sought to reject—the dualism of the saved and the damned, and the theory of afterlife rewards and punishments—has been embraced wholeheartedly by fundamentalists. The cost of this folly is not only personal and institutional isolation and disconnectedness of fundamentalist Christians from other Christians but also the alienation of humankind from the rest of creation. As fundamentalists look beyond this world toward a "new heaven and a new earth," they often forget that the world is also God's creation and that even the nonhuman world hungers for redemption (Romans 8:18–23).

Although the new age movement is denounced as demonic by fundamentalists, new age visionaries embrace the afterlife with as much fervor as their theological critics. However, the new age image of survival after death is grounded in the theory of reincarnation, the belief that this life is not our only life but that we have lived before and we will live again. Whether influenced by Hinduism, Buddhism, Theosophy, or channeled information, most adherents of new age thought would affirm that "we go on, life after life, experiencing, learning, seeking, until we have finished our course on earth and acquired all the wisdom that is to be discovered in this world."[1] Each life involves the opportunity to learn a particular lesson, which, if not learned, must be repeated in another "incarnation" until it is learned. Our personal karma, or the effects of our thoughts and actions, radiates from life to life. Who I am today, in the small and the large, is largely the result of what I have been in a previous life.

Whereas Hindus and Buddhists have often seen reincarnation as a burden to be borne or a punishment for ignorance and attachment, new age thinkers understand reincarnation optimistically. Stephen Levine states that the doctrine of karma seeks to explain the "extraordinarily simple, merciful teaching process which brings to our attention again and again those qualities that block our heart and limit our experience of full being."[2] In contrast to the traditional views that see karma and rebirth in punitive terms, Levine asserts that "karma is not punishment but an opportunity offered at level after level of experience to bring us back to balance. It is the most merciful and attentive of teachers."[3] Since the cause and effect nature of reality allows us to learn and grow, "karma is grace and grace is karmic."[4] Accordingly, as the primary mechanism of personal and global evolution, reincarnation is "an opportunity to learn all the lessons this world has to teach."[5]

However, for Christians the doctrine of reincarnation and karma presents its own moral and theological difficulties. Initially, the doctrine of karma was formulated to explain the inequities of life and the possibility of spiritual evolution. Despite its possibilities for learning "new" responses to "old" personal difficulties, the doctrine of reincarnation, as it is literally understood, may also serve as an "opiate of the masses" when it is used to explain or justify injustice in this world. My social condition, gender, and racial identity are the results of my actions in previous lives. Accordingly, it can be said that I get what I deserve, whether it be good health, economic well-being, or racial discrimination. For example, some would suggest that blacks in South Africa have "chosen" or "deserved" their present fate (perhaps, they were tyrants in a previous incarnation and now need to explore the meaning of service and injustice in this life) or that birth into an abusive family is the result of one's hardheartedness in a previous lifetime. Such interpretations of reincarnation encourage ethical complacency and suggest that injustice, brutality, and genocide have a benevolent role in the learning process. This is especially destructive since the victims of injustice—dying infants in Ethiopia, AIDS-infected babies, and teenagers in South Africa—typically have no remembrance of their past lives and, thus, can make no conscious amendment of their behaviors from a previous incarnation. Such meditation on the "wheel of life and death" has always been the luxury of those who have been sheltered from the storms of life, whether by race, economics, caste, or vocation.

Furthermore, if everyone has forever to achieve the goal of human existence, then there is no immediate need to change their life situation for the better, except insofar as it enhances their own karma. To see the incidence of cancer or the reality of oppression as merely part of a cosmic learning process is to devaluate individual suffering and render our present lives, despite the apparent significance of our karmic acts, merely a creative illusion or play, *maya*, through which the universe comes to know itself.

Despite the optimistic interpretations of karma put forth by Theosophy and the new age movements, ultimately the concept of karma is unbending, impersonal, and graceless. Karma becomes the primary energy in the cosmos. While it is obvious that the law of karma and cause and effect operate to the extent that persons choose their own destinies and reap what they have previously sown, it is equally obvious that life presents us with graceful surprises whose occurrence changes the course of even the most hardened and inflexible characters. In the course of our lives, there are times when we get more than we deserve and there are times when we get much less than we deserve. The adventure of learning, inherent in the more optimistic interpretations of karma and reincarnation, must be supplemented by a movement of grace and serendipity that allows persons to transcend their cultural, ethnic, and genetic backgrounds in surprising and unexpected ways. The concepts of karma and reincarnation cannot provide either the motivation or the support we need to transform our lives and the world.

Keeping all this in mind, I believe that it is fair to say that the skepticism of liberal Christianity receives its greatest challenge today not so much from fundamentalism or the influx of new age and Asian religions but from the recent scientific studies of "near-death experiences." Since the publication of Raymond Moody's *Life After Life*, the exploration of a postmortem existence has become an issue of science as well as faith. The work of Raymond Moody, Elisabeth Kübler-Ross, Karlis Osis, Erlendur Haraldsson, and Kenneth Ring has identified a variety of interconnected experiences, graphically described by persons at the edges of life. According to researchers, the basic elements of near-death experiences include experiences of traveling along a dark tunnel, the encounter with previously deceased companions who serve as a "welcoming committee," a review of one's past life in the company of a being of light, often identified by Christians as Jesus.[6]

With few exceptions, near-death experiences suggest that the afterlife is a time of reunion, comfort, learning, and joy. Accounts of near-death experiences suggest that eventually all persons will discern and accept the meaning of their lives. The afterlife is not seen as an escape from the problems of one's current situation. Rather, there is a continuity between one's present and future "lives" both in terms of one's companions (a person is often met by "deceased" family and friends) and one's personal history (one must reflect on one's past existence in the context of one's current postmortem existence). While research on near-death experiences does not provide conclusive evidence for survival after death, the study of such experiences nevertheless reminds religious and secular empiricists that the scope of reality greatly exceeds the limitations of our ordinary five senses.

Process metaphysics provides no reason to deny the possibility of survival after death. Furthermore, in our attempts to base theological reflection on the most general aspects of experience, process thought compels us to take into consideration not only the evidence provided by near-death experiences but also the insights of Theosophists, Hindus, "new agers," and orthodox Christians.

In the paragraphs that follow, I will articulate a process-relational vision of survival after death. I contend that any vision of the afterlife must reflect, rather than contradict, the basic principles characterizing our experience of reality. A process-relational vision of the afterlife must be understood in terms of our pervasive experience of relatedness, adventure, novelty, continuity, and openness to the divine aim.

Pushing Life's Edges: Charting the Flow into the Afterlife

A process-relational view of the afterlife is grounded in the experience of relatedness. Whereas traditional images of survival after death have emphasized individualism and isolation both in the quest for immortality and in the understanding of human destiny, a process "eschatology" (view of the "last things") maintains that the organic relatedness characteristic of our present personal and global existence must, in some way, be approximated in the afterlife.

Whitehead suggests that all experience is characterized by the interplay of spirituality, or mentality, and embodiment. Nothing in the universe is without experience or physical relationship. Even God has a "physical pole," or aspect, insofar not only as God experiences the physical world but also as God's own experience is partly characterized by memory, inheritance, and continuity between the past and the future. Whereas the "physical pole" represents the order, stability, and continuity necessary for survival, the "mental" or spiritual pole embodies the quest for novelty characteristic of adventure. Accordingly, in their symbiotic relationship, there is no sharp line between the physical and mental, either in this life or the next.

From this perspective, the primary focus of relatedness and self-identity lies in the interplay of memory, both conscious and unconscious, and novelty, characteristic of our personal existence. This interplay is possible, whether or not our lives are connected with a physical body. In human existence, self-identity involves the existence of an enduring, yet dynamic and ever-changing stream of experience characterized by the constant inheritance and transformation of the data it receives from the body, the external world, and our own previous experiences. Inheritance and relatedness are the basis for all experience, both conscious and unconscious. There can be no ongoing self, whether in the body or beyond the body, apart from repetition, stability, connectedness, and the lure of adventure, characteristic of the interplay of the physical and the mental.

Christian and Eastern eschatologies clearly affirm that life after death emerges from, and is conditioned by, one's present embodied existence. The quality of our experiences in the past and present influence the quality of future experiences, including experiences beyond the grave. Continuity rather than dislocation characterizes the relationship between the past, present, and future in this life and the next. Accordingly, there is no absolute distinction between this life and future lives. The literalist doctrines of heaven and hell perpetuate a false distinction that devaluates the pain, struggle, and significance of our current adventures. If the afterlife existence is to have any meaning in this present moment as well as beyond the grave, the thread of self-identity between our embodied and our postmortem existence must not be severed. If what I am doing today is important to me now, it must also have some importance to me beyond the grave. If we experience an absolute transformation beyond the grave in which we are suddenly perfected or damned, then our personal history and intimate relationships become peripheral and unimportant.

In contrast, process-relational metaphysics suggests that as a time of further growth and adventure, the afterlife must necessarily be characterized by healing, acceptance, and transformation of our past life as well as the discovery of new truths. While the afterlife involves a deepening and broadening of one's experience beyond the grave, these postmortem insights build upon, rather than negate, our experiences in this physical world. We carry our memories and personalities, our likes and dislikes, our gifts and talents, into the afterlife.

In a world of relationships, the past is never a solitary past, just as the future is never a solitary future. Each moment's experience arises from and contributes to the experiences of countless other drops of experience. Accordingly, the hope for future life must involve the possibility of self-knowledge, forgiveness, and repentance. At death, few persons are prepared to embrace God and our creaturely companions wholeheartedly and without reservations. We carry the bondage of "sins of omission" and "sins of commission" as well as painful memories in relation to others. To become fully open to God, others, and ourselves, we must forgive as well as be forgiven. We must transcend the sense of separateness and allow God to be "everything to everyone" (1 Corinthians 15:28), including ourselves. Until we are able to let go of the burdens of the past, we will have to confront, in various guises, those persons and behaviors that imprison us. Even Judas must allow Jesus and the other disciples to embrace and forgive him, if he is to find peace beyond the grave.

This vision of relatedness extends beyond even my own personal history and journey of forgiveness. The Christian church has often spoken of the "communion of the saints," and I believe that the communion table is not merely a feast for those present but radiates to include believers in all times and places. As the physical elements of communion manifest the universality of God's presence in all times and places, the meal also witnesses to the continuity and interrelatedness of all persons, past, present, and future. The prayers for the dead, most characteristic of the Catholic tradition, assume some level of interaction between the living and the dead. In addition to this, we have recent accounts of near-death and paranormal experiences that give evidence of communion between the living and the dead. The "welcoming committee" of friends and family as well as the information about the afterlife channeled from new age "spirit guides" suggests that all levels of existence interact with one another.

Furthermore, as the writings of the apostle Paul suggest, the "dead" may take an interest in our own well-being. In speaking of Christian hope in the face of condemnation and death, Paul proclaims not only that the risen Christ died for us but that Christ continues to pray for us (Romans 8:31–35). If Christ is the personal as well as the universal model for full humanity, then Christ's own goodwill toward our world must be mirrored in the process of sanctification beyond the grave. Our personal evolution beyond this life requires compassion toward our earthly as well as spiritual companions. Accordingly, the process of forgiveness and detachment may require the "deceased" to take an interest in the affairs of the living, especially those with whom they have forged creative or destructive bonds during their earthly existence.

The final and perhaps most important implication of a process-relational vision of survival after death is that relationships continue beyond the grave. While we must not image the afterlife in terms of our current personal lives (see Luke 20:27–39), we must assume that the images of the "reign of God" and "the heavenly city" point to the possibility of new and surprising relationships after physical death. The Hebraic and Christian image of the reign, or "kingdom," of God celebrates relatedness and love rather than solitary enjoyment as definitive of the afterlife. I believe that the afterlife is an adventure in love and inclusion.

In contrast to the church father who stated that one of the joys of heaven is to be found in "hearing the shrieks of those in hell," a relational vision of life maintains that salvation is communal and that the process of personal or cosmic salvation is not complete until alienation, brokenness, and injustice are overcome, that is, until "God may be all in all" (1 Corinthians 15:28). If the experience of personal evolution involves the expansion of consciousness, as the Christian image of the reign of God suggests, then spiritual growth beyond the grave enhances our experience of sympathy and solidarity with the totality of life. Accordingly, a process-relational vision of survival after death responds to Charles Hartshorne's critique of individual salvation. Salvation is not a personal possession but a shared experience—the sanctification of one requires the sanctification of the totality. The reign of God cannot be found alone.

A process-relational vision of the afterlife recognizes that all experience involves adventure, novelty, and the prospect of evolutionary growth. In contrast to the vision of the afterlife as a static and monotonous experience (for example, the popular myth of eternal flames or eternal harp-playing), process thought envisions the afterlife in terms of dynamic change and lively self-discovery. A process vision affirms and reinterprets the deeper insights of the doctrines of reincarnation and purgatory. While neither doctrine should be taken literally, both reflect the insight that this life as well as any future life is a process of growth and learning, guided by the ideals of acceptance, transformation, and inclusion.

While this continuity of life implies that there are no sharp breaks between our present and future lives, it also affirms the possibility of a heightened experience of grace and self-awareness in the afterlife. There are lessons to be learned. Yet, in contrast to the literal doctrine of karma and reincarnation, these lessons are facilitated by the presence of a graceful and supportive environment, and a graceful and supportive God. A process-relational vision of the afterlife integrates the traditional images of sanctification or "growing in grace," on the one hand, with the new age image of personal evolution, on the other hand. In a world of relationships, one's afterlife journey may be nurtured by "helpers," "guardian spirits," or "angels" as well as "deceased" loved ones. Unimpeded by apparent boundaries between differing dimensions of reality, one now may have direct communion with higher beings, whose purpose is to stimulate our experience of God's aim toward beauty, harmony, and reconciliation.

This understanding of the afterlife also avoids the moral problems suggested by the Marxist critique. In affirming the continuity of life and the relatedness of one's present experience to one's future destiny, a relational vision affirms that this life as well as one's afterlife existence is important. Indeed, our present and future lives are different only in degree and not in kind. Each plane of existence is an environment in which we are called to learn the meaning of creative and responsive love. Our commitment to fostering beauty of experience in this life not only contributes to our own future selves but to God and the ongoing universe. To seek justice and to nurture beauty today is to make a contribution to this world and the next, to one's own destiny as well as to the destiny of all other beings. In a world in which being and doing are united, personal self-affirmation and self-acceptance contribute to the self-affirmation and self-acceptance of one's partners in the cosmic adventure. Accordingly, there is ultimately no distinction between authentic self-interest and the welfare of others. Indeed, as the Christian tradition has maintained, to love God, oneself, and the neighbor selflessly is the primary path to joy and fulfillment in this life and the next. As the Westminster Catechism proclaims, we are to glorify God and also to enjoy God forever.

A process-relational vision of the afterlife affirms that God's role in the afterlife is consistent in aim and character with God's role in our present existence. God is with us always. Process thought affirms the biblical insight that God's love for the world is both creative and receptive. God creates the world and influences each moment of experience through the presentation of ideal possibilities, congruent with each person's unique history, environment, and values. God's aim toward the highest possibility for any given drop of experience is governed by God's quest for beauty, adventure, and the complexity of experience. Paul's affirmation that nothing "in all creation, will be able to separate us from the love of God in Christ Jesus our Lord" (Romans 8:39) is a witness to God's enduring faithfulness even beyond the grave. In God's experience, love is stronger than death. The God who accompanies us at the edges of life, presenting us with possibilities for transformation, experiencing our pain and struggle, does not abandon us at the moment of death. In whatever adventures we have beyond the grave, God will be present in a manner similar to God's presence in this life. God will share our experiences and challenge us with new possibilities as we participate in the dynamic movement of the reign of God.

The afterlife provides novel and undreamed of possibilities for growth and self-discovery. Truly, God will be doing a "new thing" in our lives. "Now we see in a mirror, dimly, but then we will see face to face" (1 Corinthians 13:12). As we grow in grace and in expansiveness of vision, unimaginable possibilities will become relevant to our experience.

Even in the afterlife, however, we possess an element of freedom and self-determination that allows us to respond to God's aims for us in our own unique and surprising ways. Since God's grace is always persuasive in character, the tension between divine action and human freedom that plagues some formulations of the doctrine of universal salvation is absent from a process-relational vision of the afterlife. Although God abandons no one, God's loving presence—even in the afterlife—is conditioned by our creaturely responses. We are neither puppets nor robots. We can say "no" to the good news time after time. We can create our own hell. Nevertheless, every creaturely "no" and every creaturely "hell" is countered by the divine "yes" and the "heavenly vision." While it is our hope that all beings will eventually embrace God's grace in all its dimensions, there is neither an absolute timetable nor a final day of judgment. Nor is there any one specific model for fully actualized existence. To "live in Christ" does not mean uniformity, either of experience or of goal. It does mean, however, that we experience God's presence in the way that most fits our own personal history and vocation. With the expansion of self-awareness and cosmic sympathy, some persons may feel called to become "guides" or "guardian angels" to their earthly counterparts, while others may choose to become "helpers" to other afterlife adventurers. In a world of relationships, the progress of other adventurers on their journey toward God contributes to our own enjoyment and personal growth.

Although a process vision of the afterlife abandons literal interpretations of the doctrines of hell and karma, it affirms their insight that our earthly decisions are significant both for ourselves and for others. Full communion with God, others, and ourselves is often a long and circuitous journey. But at each moment, God is present to guide, comfort, and challenge the pilgrim on his way. The dynamics of the divine-human relationship do not change in the afterlife. The God who guides is also the One who receives all our experiences. God experiences us not only as we were but as we are. What we do beyond the grave not only contributes to the quality of God's experience but also enables God to respond to the world as well as to ourselves in new and imaginative ways.

We cannot speculate on the ultimate destination of our journeys. Whether our ultimate destiny involves unity with God or continuing personal existence or both, it is clear that the enlightenment and sanctification we seek as the highest good in earthly life is an essential element of the life to come. Process thought does not see the loss of personal existence as the highest spiritual goal. Rather a process vision of the afterlife sees transformation, expansion, and beauty as primary goals in this life and the next. Our destiny is to become "little Christs" through whom the love of God flows. Here, authentic peace or *shalom* becomes our experience and our gift. Adventure is joined with grace and peace. Whitehead's description of peace rightly describes the goal and the motivation of the human adventure in this life and the next:

> Peace carries with it the surpassing of personality....Peace is the removal of inhibition and not its introduction. It results in a wider sweep of conscious interest. It enlarges the field of conscious attention. Thus peace is self-control at its widest,—at the width where the self has been lost and interest has been transferred to coordinations wider than personality.[7]

Conclusion

As we face the edges of our lives and look beyond toward vague and uncharted horizons, the ultimate inspiration for our adventures is love—the love we feel for others, the love of beauty, the love we struggle to experience as we face ourselves, and through it all the love of God that is our companion in every moment of living and of dying. In love alone is found peace and enlightenment. For as we grow in love, we experience both our roots and our destiny in divinity. We discover that love, in its cosmic and creaturely forms, is the only healer. As we make the daily adventure of living and dying, we will discover that this omnipresent love is stronger than death and that "each tree and leaf and star show how the universe is part of this one cry, that every life is noted and is cherished, and that nothing loved is ever lost or perished."[8]

In Dostoyevski's *The Brothers Karamazov*, the young monk Alyosha mourns the death of his spiritual teacher, Father Zossima. In the midst of the funeral, Alyosha becomes fearful as he envisages the wedding feast of God. In the midst of his fear, he hears the voice of Father Zossima comforting him, "Do not fear Him.

He is terrible in his greatness, awful in his sublimity, but infinitely merciful. He has made himself like unto us from love and rejoices with us." Suddenly Alyosha's eyes are opened.

The vault of heaven, full of soft shining stars stretched vast and formless above him. The Milky Way ran in two pale streams from the zenith to the horizon. The fresh, motionless, still night enfolded the earth....The silence of the earth seemed to melt into the silence of the heavens. The mystery of the earth was one with the mystery of the stars. Alyosha stood, gazed and suddenly threw himself down on the earth....He kissed it weeping, sobbing and watering it with his tears, and vowed passionately to love it, to love it forever and ever. "Water the earth with the tears of your joy and love those tears," echoed in his soul....

There seemed to be threads from all those innumerable worlds of God, linking his soul to everyone of them....He longed to forgive everyone and for everything, and to beg forgiveness. Oh, not for himself, but for all men, for all and for everything....

He had fallen to earth a weak boy, but he rose up a resolute champion....And never, never, all his life long, could Alyosha forget that moment.[9]

At the edges of life, we find that there is an everlasting love in all things that cries and rejoices with us, leading us to even greater adventure yet to come.

Notes

[1]John Algeo, *Reincarnation Explored* (Wheaton, Illinois: Quest Books, 1987), p. 1.

[2]Stephen Levine, *Healing into Life and Death* (New York: Doubleday, 1987) p. 34.

[3]*Ibid.*

[4]*Ibid.*, p. 35.

[5]Algeo, *Reincarnation Explored*, 1987.

[6]For further study, see Raymond Moody, *Life After Life* (New York: Bantam, 1975); Karlis Osis and Erlendur Haraldsson, *At the Hour of Death* (New York: Avon, 1977); Kenneth Ring, *Life at Death*, (New York: Coward, McCann, & Geoghegan, 1980) and *Heading Towards Omega* (New York: Morrow, 1984).

[7]Whitehead, *Adventures of Ideas*, p. 287.

[8]L'Engle, *A Ring of Endless Light*, p. 172.

[9]Fyodor Dostoyevski, *The Brothers Karamazov* (New York: Random House, 1950), pp. 435-437.